FROM HIRED
TO HAPPY

THE SECRETS TO A VIBRANT CAREER
AND A FULFILLING LIFE

FROM HIRED TO HAPPY

THE SECRETS TO A VIBRANT CAREER AND A FULFILLING LIFE

Ruth Gerath

Hyde Street Publishing

MASSACHUSETTS · MAINE

This book is published as a general reference and not intended to be a substitute for independent verification by readers. It is sold with the understanding that neither the author nor publisher is engaged in rendering any legal, psychological, or accounting advice. The resources listed in this book are not referrals. The author and/or publisher shall have neither liability nor responsibility to any person or entity with respect to any loss or damage caused, or alleged to be caused, directly or indirectly by the information contained in this book. If you do not wish to be bound by the above, you may return this publication to the seller for a full refund.

Publisher's Cataloging In Publication
Gerath, Ruth
From hired to happy: the secrets to a vibrant career and a fulfilling life / Ruth Gerath.

      p. cm.
      Includes bibliographical references and index.
      LCCN 2010912750
      ISBN-13: 978-0-9844496-0-6
      ISBN-10: 0-9844496-0-4

      1. Success. 2. Success in business. 3. Happiness.
      4. Self-actualization (Psychology) I. Title.

BF637.S8G47 2011   158.1
                               QBI10-600173

ATTN: QUANTITY DISCOUNTS ARE AVAILABLE TO YOUR COMPANY OR EDUCATIONAL INSTITUTION
For more information, please contact the publisher at:

Hyde Street Publishing
Acton, Massachusetts 01720
Phone: 978-263-3060
success@gerath.com

Interior Design by: William Groetzinger

For my mother, who encouraged me to write; for my father, who told me I could do anything I put my mind to; and for Chris, who believed them.

"I've spent my career watching smart people blow themselves up. I wrote *From Hired to Happy* to reduce the carnage."

—Ruth Gerath

CONTENTS

Introduction

"They say that time changes things, but you
actually have to change them yourself."
—Andy Warhol

This book was written to help you make the most of whatever you are doing, or wherever you are, in work and life. It's about maximizing your assets—starting with your mind—because how you think, feel, and act has everything to do with what happens in your life and your career. Once you understand that concept, and have a few simple techniques under your belt, you will be capable of creating much, much more of what you want, and a whole lot less of what you don't.

From Hired to Happy is about moving beyond just going through the paces to being actively and satisfyingly involved in your work and outside of it. In other words, it's about going from simply being in a job (hired) to interested, engaged, and maybe even fulfilled (happy) at work.

Do any of these situations apply to you?

- You've been in a job for some time and things have become stale. You just can't seem to muster the enthusiasm you once had.

- You are starting a new position, making a fresh start, and want to give yourself every opportunity to succeed right out of the gate.

- You are searching for work and know you need to make a positive impact during interviews.

- You are a leader and want your team to have the skills they need to be top performers with winning attitudes.

The techniques and skills described in the following chapters will be as effective in your career as they will be in your personal life. You are not two people: one at work, the other away from work. You are one. How you think, how you feel, and ultimately how you act at work is the same as how you think, feel, and act outside of it.

Most (or at least many) people live out their lives believing the notion that life happens. Well, life does happen. But what kind of a life and what kind of a career experience do you want? And what are you doing to create it? You have the ability to increase your career success and personal well-being. You just might not know how to do it yet, even if you've been in an established career. That is what you will learn in the chapters that follow.

You will read stories about people just like you who have found ways to make their work situations better and, therefore, improve their level of satisfaction and success. They have learned how to take a challenging situation and use it to grow and become happier because of it, and you will too.

You will also learn what positive psychology has revealed and how using scientifically proven, easy to do, and enjoyable techniques can transform your life and your work experience. In order to provide research in this fascinating field, I had the great privilege of taking Dr. Tal Ben-Shahar's course in Positive Psychology from the University of Pennsylvania. Dr. Ben-Shahar is a passionate proponent of the life-changing effects of positive psychology, and he's a tremendously talented teacher.

The idea for writing *From Hired to Happy* came out of my many years working for and with companies from Fortune 10s to small entrepreneurial organizations in a wide variety of industries. I worked for IBM for many years, then for a large financial institution, before moving into consulting, where I've had clients from across the globe. No matter the size of the organization, one thing is true: Everyone who works there is human (so far), which means that from the largest to the smallest companies, the issues, challenges, and dynamics that go on every day are remarkably similar. Why? Because we all think, feel, and act. That's it. Get a handle on how to do those three things in a conscious and effective way and, look out, things can change instantly.

Ultimately, I wanted to write a book that would help people in the workplace because I've seen a lot of pain and suffering. I've known lots of smart people who are trying hard yet are miserable with their situations. I wanted to give people practical and instantly implementable skills so that they could take control of their situations and create more positive, productive, and successful outcomes.

The techniques in *From Hired to Happy* have the power to change organizations as well as individuals. Imagine a team of highly responsible people with strong, positive attitudes, great listening skills, and respect for each other. Wow. No list of external incentives could best that kind of environment. If you are a leader, these skills are for you and for your team.

I believe that there is a drive to find a new approach to work and life: a paradigm shift from the old approach of having one life at work and another at home. The desire now is to integrate the two. And it's about time!

In *From Hired to Happy,* I hope to show that you have a lot more control over your career, and your life, than you might have previously thought, and that with consistent application of a few new skills, you can make a significant, lasting, and enjoyable difference in your career and in your life.

HOW TO USE THIS BOOK

In Part One, "The Foundation," you will learn about the three levels of happiness, how to manage your emotions so that they don't derail you, and simple strategies to create a higher level of lasting happiness over time.

In Part Two, "Success Traits," you will learn why becoming a pragmatic optimist is necessary for building a successful career and a happy life. You will explore how to make the most of your network, set and achieve your goals, take full responsibility for yourself, and focus on your strengths—all very important skills for professional success and personal well-being.

Part Three, "Big-Picture Skills," is about creating strong listening and speaking skills, dealing effectively with people you find challenging, building your moral compass, and coping with change in a healthy way. Again, all of these are skills that will help you take your career and your personal relationships to the next level.

In order to learn anything, you need time to reflect on what you've heard, read, or seen. The "Take a Minute" boxes contain questions designed to apply the concepts to your own experience.

I've attempted to create a soup-to-nuts approach that covers the many elements of building a successful career and personal satisfaction and well-being. I wanted to create one place to go for a lot of important information that you will use throughout your career. Reading *From Hired to Happy* may be all that you require, or it may be a jumping-off point for more intensive study. Many of these chapters could be (and are) the subjects of entire books. There are many wonderful books and research articles if this is your interest. You can find a number of them in the Resources at the end of the book.

So let's start at the beginning and find what really makes us happy. See you in Chapter One.

PART ONE: THE FOUNDATION

"Most people are about as happy
as they make up their minds to be."
—Abraham Lincoln

1

What Happiness Is and Isn't

"There is no duty so underrated as the duty
of being happy. By being happy we sow
anonymous benefits upon the world."
—Robert Louis Stevenson

THE BACK STORY

What is it that you most want from your career? Is it to have an exciting and rewarding experience, to work with great people who inspire you, to help others, to make a lot of money, to achieve prestige, to cure cancer, to have a stable job that is satisfying and supports your lifestyle?

Whatever you want, two things are certain: first, you need the right skills to achieve your goals, and second, they aren't all about the job.

What do I mean?

Let me tell you a story.

In the dark ages of the 1980s, I had the good fortune to be hired by IBM. I say that my fortune was good because then, as now, IBM is one the best companies in the world to work for. My parents, both the first in their families to go to college, were thrilled; their daughter had made it to the holy grail of companies. All their hard work, discipline, and sacrifices were paying off.

Soon after I started the job, I was on the first of what would become many flights from Boston, where I lived, to Texas, where IBM had a training center. Over the next year, my newly hired colleagues and I learned how to become professionals. We had lessons in the latest (now oh-so-long-ago) technologies, how to work with customers, and how to demonstrate products and give presentations.

We also had classes on how to dress for success, which for women consisted of suits with mid-knee-length skirts, preferably from Brooks Brothers, and little bow-tie things that I can say without hesitation did not look good on anyone. And we learned about business ethics.

That education became the foundation for my career. It was priceless—and rare. Today millions of people in companies of all sizes across the globe are expected to know what to do in order to be professional and therefore open one of the most important doors to career success. But if these skills aren't taught, then how, and where, can they be learned? It's the rare organization that provides training in professional skill development to employees. And although most colleges and universities prepare students for job interviews, they do not train them on what to expect, what to do, and, often more importantly, what not to do once they are employed.

I worked for IBM for twelve years. After that I held positions with a major financial institution, then was part of a team that built a publicly traded consulting firm, and in 2003 I started my own company.

PARADISE LOST—AND FOUND

Beneath the surface of what looked like the start of a successful career, another story was playing out. Depression runs in my family and so, not surprisingly given this genetic predisposition, this dark demon came calling on me when I was in my twenties. Each success was met with an equal amount of anxiety. What if I couldn't keep up with the work? Maybe I'd just been lucky to get promoted. I found it almost impossible to simply enjoy the experiences.

The pain and frustration of being unhappy at best, depressed at worst, and having several long but ultimately unsuccessful relationships led me on a journey to find a solution to my problem. I wanted a better life, one that was successful both on the outside and on the inside.

Although this was an extremely challenging experience, it was also a time of growth. I learned skills that opened a whole new world to me. I let go of the belief that I was a victim of my genetics, or my thoughts, and discovered that I had a huge amount of control over how I felt and how I reacted to situations both at work and in my personal life. I dedicated myself to figuring out how to live happily and healthily, and to continue to build my career at the same time. It was a period of intense self-discovery, at the end of which I met and married my husband of twenty years now.

This led me on a path that resulted in the part of this book that focuses on happiness, because once I got beyond depression, I realized that I wanted even more. The lack of pain was just the first step. I wanted to be happy. I wanted to be able to pursue a career that would be increasingly challenging and rewarding. My goal was to be able to tackle those challenges without having them knock me for an emotional loop. I believed that I could have more than just the absence of pain. I could take risks, face trouble, experience self-doubt occasionally, and find a way to bounce back to a happy state relatively quickly. And that's what I found and what I want to share with you. This book has a blend of the professional skills I learned early on (and have honed by managing organizations for many years) and the strategies that have helped me become happier and more resilient.

THE EMERGENCE OF POSITIVE PSYCHOLOGY

About forty years ago a group of psychologists decided that it was important to study the positive side of the human experience. Prior to that, for many good reasons that included helping returning veterans from World War II deal with the trauma of war, psychology research was based almost entirely on understanding and curing pathologies—the things that make us psychologically and emotionally unwell. A lot of research has been done in this area, resulting in effective medications and therapies for a wide variety of psychological illnesses. However, the same amount of research has not been done on understanding our strengths and positive traits.

In 1998 Martin Seligman became the president of the American Psychological Association and, under his guidance, positive psychology began to flourish. This scientific approach to studying optimal human functioning took hold and is gaining increased steam through the efforts of a growing group of psychologists dedicated to learning and teaching what makes us happier and more resilient. And so far they've done a great job of it, as evidenced by the results from research projects that show very clearly how we can improve our lives by practicing happiness-increasing skills.

IS IT OKAY TO WANT TO BE HAPPY?

"Happiness is the meaning and purpose of life,
the whole aim and end of human existence."

—Aristotle

Have you ever wondered if it is appropriate to want to be happy? After all, there are lots of bad situations and suffering going on in the world. Isn't it selfish to want more happiness in light of these things? And how on earth can you expect to be happy at work when there are day-to-day challenges and unforeseen situations around each corner?

All true. There is a great deal of suffering in the world and work can be challenging and unpredictable. But that does not mean that there is value in being unhappy. People who are happy spread the wealth of their positive states, which in turn makes others happier. This is a pay-it-forward concept. Try it sometime. Just walk into a store with a smile on your face and say hello to the first person you meet. See if you don't get a smile in return. Or think about someone you know who is usually genuinely upbeat and positive, yet grounded in reality. How do you feel when you are with him or her?

HOW BEING HAPPIER HELPS YOU SUCCEED

Being happy is a career enhancer because people like to work with genuinely happy people. We all like to be around the energy and enthusiasm, and the can-do, solution-oriented attitudes that happiness creates.

In other words, people like to work with people they like. And it's easier to like someone who is optimistic, collaborative, and respectful of others—all of which are traits that lead to being lastingly happy, as we will see in the rest of this book.

Genuinely happy people are more resilient than unhappy people. Simply stated, they bounce back from hardships more quickly than others. This is an ability that brings great benefits in the workplace. If you can move through a challenging situation without going for a ride on an emotional roller coaster, you will be much more effective and better able to handle increasing responsibly.

Research shows that naturally happy people have built-in resilience and that each of us can increase our level of happiness by practicing the skills these statistical outliers were born with. To that end, practicing the skills in this book will help you to:

- *Manage your career* with confidence.
- *Become more attractive* to employers.
- *Seek out, and find, resources* that can help you achieve your goals (and to ask for what you want and need).
- *Use your network* in a powerful way.
- *Be more giving and helpful* to others and receive the benefits in return.
- *Express your gratitude* easily and openly, which helps build strong alliances at work.
- *Savor the small successes* and joys.

But there's more to be gained from the pursuit of happiness at work. A 2002 study showed that even without an initial advantage of wealth, college freshmen that were happy earned higher salaries sixteen years later.

TAKE A MINUTE

00:01:00 Think of a time in your life when you have been happy. What were you doing, who were you with, where were you? What about the situation made you happy?

HAPPINESS IN PERSPECTIVE

Positive psychology shows that happiness is experienced on three levels:

1. Pleasure
2. Engagement
3. Meaning

Let's look at each a bit more closely.

PLEASURE. This is called the hedonic level of happiness. It's the happiness you experience when you get a new car, for example. At first it smells great, drives wonderfully, and is a thrill every time you get into it. You can't wait to get up in the morning and drive to work because you'll be in your fabulous new vehicle. But within a few months (sometimes less), you go back to being as happy as you were before you got your new car.

ENGAGEMENT. This is when you are involved in some-thing that engages you fully. Say, for example, you're working on a project that requires intense concen-tration and focus. You feel good about what you are doing and what you are accomplishing. It allows you to experience what psychologists call "flow."

MEANING. This is the highest level of happiness, and it is experienced when you are using your strengths to be in the service of something larger than your-self. This is where you experience purpose in life.

As we go through life, we experience all three of these levels of happiness. Pleasure, although cer-tainly a source of positive emotions, is the most short-lived of the levels. This is one reason why after the initial high of getting a new job, for example, we can rather quickly return to whatever level of happi-ness we experienced before.

The chart that follows illustrates what happens when we get a boost in happiness from the purchase of something new, or a raise, or a new job.

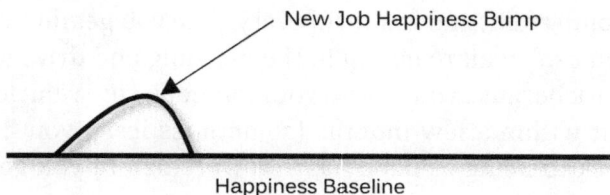

New Job Happiness Bump

Happiness Baseline

When we get a new job, for example, we experience a bump in happiness. But not too long afterward, we return to the base level we were at before the new position.

NOT HAPPY OR UNHAPPY

Many people live in a state that is neither unhappy nor happy. They aren't depressed, nor do they experience a sense of joy or happiness. The result is that they live their lives (and work their work) by just going through the motions.

How can this be when there is so much around to keep one amused and entertained? The answer lies in the levels of happiness. If the only way you can feel happiness is to experience stimulation from an outside source, and we've seen that this is a fleeting experience, then you are doomed to keep reaching for more of the same.

Once basic needs are met (food, clothing, shelter), income doesn't contribute much to satisfaction with life. That's not to say you should quit your job and move to a remote corner of the Earth because money doesn't really mean anything. Actually, that would be, for most people, a counterproductive move because naturally happy people have strong ties to friends and family.

Having a solid career and a good income is a laudable goal. It can enable you to have much that life has to offer, and there is nothing wrong with wanting that. However, if the sole focus of your work and your life is to amass more and more things, and bigger and better things, without seeking activities that are engaging and meaningful to you, and without developing strong social connections—well, lasting happiness may be difficult to find.

BALANCING THINGS OUT

The good news in all of this is that once you become aware there are levels of happiness, and what they are and how they work, you can choose to participate in activities that will enable you to spend more time in the higher levels. This is something you have a lot of control over, as you will see in the following chapters.

STORY

MOVING UP THE HAPPINESS LADDER

Six years ago I decided it was time for a change. I knew I loved being active professionally and working with interesting clients and challenging situations, but how this new phase of my career would play out—well, I just wasn't sure.

The change I wanted wasn't all about work. I wanted to spend more time doing things that I had put on the back burner for years—way too many years. But that thought was daunting. How on earth was I going to incorporate those things while at the same time building a new career, and ultimately a new business? Wouldn't I just fall into my old ways of working sixty to eighty hours a week, too exhausted at the end for anything more than going out for a nice dinner with my husband and reading the Sunday paper?

I wasn't looking for work–life balance—a concept that I don't subscribe to. I don't even know what it means really, since we are constantly making trade-offs: less work, more time, less money—that kind of thing.

What I wanted was to be happier. That was the simple goal. I wanted to spend more time each day doing things that gave me a sense of joy and satisfaction, and that I could lose myself in. At the time I didn't know anything about positive psychology, or the levels of happiness. I just knew that although I still wanted and needed to work, I also wanted, and on a deep, personal level needed, to move myself into a direction of incorporating more things into my life that were satisfying and made me happy. I figured that if I could do that, the rest would work itself out. And it did.

Often it seemed like I was groping in the dark. I had to constantly give myself permission to do things like go for a walk, which would get me away from my office and into the out-of-doors world where I would feel refreshed. And as I walked more regularly, I became increasingly aware of my surroundings—the movement of the clouds in the sky, the birds making a lovely racket as they played, the buds emerging on the trees in the spring. How could it be that I had missed these lovely and soul-nourishing things that were literally right outside my door?

From that humble start I began adding other activities that were deeply satisfying, including reestablishing relationships with friends and colleagues that I'd long put off seeing. Next was to take a coaching course because I wanted to add that to my skill set. During that experience I met someone who has become a dear friend and colleague.

As time went, on I continued to keep myself focused on the list of things I needed to do every day. I've taken courses, joined professional clubs, hosted several family reunions (a whole other topic), and written a book—which has been a remarkable journey in itself.

And it started with one driving desire: to be genuinely happy.

—My story

TAKE A MINUTE

[00:01:00   What do you do that makes you happy?

What level of happiness do they fall in?]

CHAPTER HIGHLIGHTS · CHAPTER HIGHLIGHTS · CHAPTER HIGHLIGHTS

Becoming happier has a pay-it-forward impact because happy people make other people happier.

The three levels of happiness are all valid, but as you go from pleasure to engagement to meaning, you will experience longer-lasting happiness.

2

You Can Become Happier

"Your beliefs become your thoughts, your thoughts become your words, your words become your actions, your actions become your habits, your habits become your destiny."

—Mahatma Gandhi

FORTY PERCENT BELONGS TO YOU

In *The How of Happiness,* Sonja Lyubomirsky shows that we have a lot more control over our happiness than we might think. Her research shows that 50 percent of our lasting happiness is determined by our happiness set point (like a weight set point),

10 percent from circumstances, and a whopping 40 percent of how happy we are is determined by what we do to make ourselves so.

This is great news. It means that you do not have to be a slave to your emotions, and that you can, by making in some cases small changes, feel happier and therefore reap the rewards that this brings.

DON'T BELIEVE EVERYTHING YOU THINK

"A man who is master of himself can end a sorrow as easily as he can invent a pleasure. I don't want to be at the mercy of my emotions. I want to use them, to enjoy them, and to dominate them."

—Oscar Wilde

When you have a thought, it is the start of a cascade. Actually, the real start is an event that causes you to have a thought. Once the thought occurs, it generates an emotion. And from the emotion, action is taken.

| EVENT | THOUGHT | EMOTION | ACTION |

Without awareness, many people simply act out of emotion. Someone says something unkind to you, and you feel hurt and then act on that emotion. You might withdraw from the source of your pain, yell at the person that said the hurtful words, or attack back. None of which usually comes to good end.

So when you stop and ask yourself what you are feeling, what thought preceded the emotion, what is an equally true but different thought that will make you feel better, you are well on your way to changing your actions to something that will be in your best interest (and the best interest of others).

The real value of this exercise is in its cumulative effect. By doing this regularly, you will spend more time experiencing positive emotions and less time feeling negative ones. This creates a foundation of positivity on which you will respond to future situations. Basically, the more genuinely positive emotions you experience, the more likely you are to feel positively in the future. You are building your emotional house on a solid footing of positivity based on positive thoughts.

In this next story we will see how these concepts were put to use to change a difficult situation into a winning one.

STORY

GETTING CLEAR

> About five years ago I was very, very unhappy. I would literally put my hand on the doorknob of my office and stress would flow through my body. I would think, *I don't want to be here—* I was so unhappy. I couldn't figure out what had shifted. There wasn't a big demarcation

of something that I could put my finger on. *What's the difference here?* I asked myself.

I decided to play a little mental game with myself and take note every time that I was doing something that made me happy and when I was back to the energized, enthusiastic person I had been. Then I thought I'd also take note of the things that make me crazy. But I realized, *No, no, no. That will make me crazy, so let's try to find the things that make me happy and focus on those things.* I was so afraid that I'd gotten to burnout—real burnout—and I was going to have to make a drastic change in my life.

So that was the epiphany I had one day over breakfast. Then, later that morning I was driving to see a client, and right away something popped up: I realized that I liked driving to see my client. I had this eager anticipation about what we were working on. I thought *Hmm, that's interesting.* And then I got to my client's and it was fun and fulfilling, just as I'd anticipated it to be in the car. I thought, *That's good—I do still like working with clients.*

A day later I met with a prospect and I immediately connected with him. I was a bit apprehensive because I wasn't sure it would work out, but in the background I was thinking, *I like doing this even if he doesn't hire me; I like what I'm doing.*

That afternoon I was inspecting some work to prepare to give feedback on so we could make changes and present it to the client. I was inspecting the work by myself, just looking at the work, and I thought, *I'm proud of what we deliver; I think it's good,* and I made the mental note that that was nice too.

Then I was going to give the feedback to a couple of my employees, and at that moment, the hair on the back of my neck stood up and it hit me: I like my job, I love working with clients, I like prospecting, it's part of what I do—it *is* what I do—but what I don't like is doing other people's jobs and paying them for it. I got real clear that it wasn't my job, my functionality, my task, and the purpose in what I do. The team I was working with had lost their fire, and they didn't care anymore.

They were doing their job in a half-baked way, and I was doing the other half of their work (and paying them for it), which really made it clear what had to change. Very clear.

So I started to figure out how I was going to reorganize my company and make changes. I realized most of the problems were coming from my second lieutenant because she was so not engaged; she was polluting the air. She was someone I really trusted and was therefore somebody you didn't complain about because I didn't want to hear it. I had a blind spot. She wasn't really doing her job and I was covering for her—and I didn't realize I was doing it. And there were so many critical things I dealt with that I was fearful of letting her go and I thought, *Well, who is going to do that?* But when I got strength from my positive thinking about what I like and don't like, I realized that I would just figure it out. I figured out how to start this company, so I could figure out how to get through this. And so I lost my fear; the pain overtook my fear.

I gave her the news that I was letting her go, and she left ten minutes after that, so I was stuck holding the bag. I went through the office—it took me about two weeks to figure out exactly where things were—and I started making changes in processes. As I was cleaning and talking about what we were going to do and not do now, everyone took note that this is how things are going to be. Everyone got focused and energized.

I use this method of self-evaluation regularly now when I start to think that I'm over here and then realize that I'm not so far from where I want to be.

—President of a branding and design firm

TAKE A MINUTE

`00:01:00` Think of and write about a time when you were feeling bad. How might you have changed what you were thinking, and what might you have felt as a result?

THE RESILIENCE FACTOR

The ability to bounce back rather than be caught in a prolonged downslide from the many challenges and hardships that life can present is called *resilience*. It is the ability to withstand life's challenges and rebound fairly quickly. This mental and emotional pliability is extremely important for career development. Why? Because as you may have experienced, the work environment is loaded with challenges, some of which can derail even the strongest career.

The process of questioning and potentially replacing your thoughts with something that is equally true but that makes you feel more hopeful and optimistic is an important component of creating happiness, which results in greater resilience.

CREATING NEW NEURAL PATHWAYS

In Marci Schimoff's wonderful book, *Happy for No Reason,* she states scientists have discovered that each day we think, on average, about 60,000 thoughts and that 95 percent of them are the same thoughts we had yesterday, and will have tomorrow. Now here's the thing: 80 percent of them are negative. That means that, every day, you are likely to be thinking 45,000 negative thoughts.

That's a lot of negative thoughts. And the problem is that these negative, and often automatic, thoughts are drainers, stealing a bit of your precious energy each time they ramble along their well-worn path, the neural pathway. Here are some sample negative zappers:

"I'm never going to get this done."

"This outfit looks hideous on me."

"He's getting all the praise and I'm doing all the work."

"This is endless."

"No one respects how hard I work."

"I'm not paid enough for what I do."

No wonder we get upset, angry, depressed, and ultimately discouraged when we are essentially hitting ourselves over the head all day long with thoughts that make us feel bad.

As daunting as it seems, you can get control of these thoughts, and by doing so, change them to equally true ones that make you feel energized and enthusiastic.

YOU GOTTA FEEL IT

This leads me to something of a fine point: Sometimes it's completely okay and cathartic to have a good rant. Many times I've done just that (in the privacy of my own home, of course). And once I was done, I could take a much cooler approach to the situation.

Say, for example, someone did something that you really didn't like. Maybe she was critical of your work, which you happened to think was close to a Picasso painting in quality. Worse, she showed her distain in front of others.

This kind of situation is painful, and it's important to let yourself feel pain, just as it's important to feel love, empathy, and joy. When we don't allow ourselves to feel, when we push down the experience of painful emotions, we are destined to relive them over and over. So let yourself experience everything that life has to offer—for a while. The trick is to really feel it and then move on.

Once a long time ago, I experienced a painful ending to a relationship that meant a great deal to me. My life was suddenly turned upside down. Rather than allow myself to experience the pain, I poured myself into my work and social activities. But I was miserable.

One day a friend took me aside and told me a story about what she'd learned during a difficult divorce. She said that after months of trying to squelch the pain and hurt, she finally gave in to it. She went home on a Friday night with a bunch of old movies and a journal. She had purposefully chosen movies that would make her think of her ex. All weekend she watched movies, cried, screamed into a pillow, and wrote in her journal.

On Monday morning she returned to work in a different frame of mind. Although she wasn't happy, she also didn't have that feeling of deadness inside. She could imagine someday feeling better, even happy again.

After my friend told me her story, I did the same thing, and experienced the same results. It took time to heal, but at least at the end of one very Kleenex-soaked weekend, I was no longer an emotional zombie.

PUT MEANING INTO PERSPECTIVE

A man came upon two workers breaking granite, so he stopped to ask them, "What are you doing?" The first one sarcastically replied, "What does it look like I'm doing? I'm trying to break this granite." The second worker enthusiastically responded, "I'm part of a team of people who are building a beautiful cathedral."

In the last chapter we explored the three levels of happiness: pleasure, engagement, and meaning. Pleasure comes from hedonic experiences (a new car, a new job) and is transitory, engagement comes from being deeply involved in what you are doing and experiencing flow, and meaning comes from the experience of being in service of something greater than yourself. Well, if meaning is the highest level of happiness, then let's all go for that, right? Actually, it's a wonderful goal and one that you can work on from any point in your life.

The story above about the two stonecutters is a wonderful illustration of how to do this. Who do you think is happier; the worker who saw his job as just breaking granite or the other who saw himself as part of a team building a beautiful structure?

FINDING MEANING IN CLEANING

On the second day of an unanticipated stay in the hospital, a man, Louis, came into my room to prepare the bed next to mine for a patient who would arrive shortly from surgery.

He moved energetically around the room, stripping the bed, removing the mattress, and washing down everything in sight. Then he started to talk. Louis had a lot to say, and I was happy to listen as he attacked his work with gusto.

Louis had two children, a little boy and a younger girl. He worked two jobs to support them because his wife could not work; she had to stay home to take care of their daughter, who had been born with a severe spinal defect and could not walk.

Scrubbing and rinsing and scrubbing some more, Louis told me how important his work was. He had to make absolutely sure that the facilities were free of germs so that the patients could heal without getting infections. "See how we do it?" he said turning the mattress over and washing the top, bottom, and all four sides. Louis showed me with pride the quality of his work.

As he worked, Louis told me about his family; how he and his wife had helped build homes for Habitat for Humanity and how, after many years of being on the list for a home themselves, they finally received one. He was thrilled that it was built to accommodate his daughter's wheelchair. His daughter, he said, laughing, is very funny and is always making her parents laugh.

When he was almost finished cleaning the room, Louis told me that sometimes he thought he might like to move to Florida but that he never would move because he was so grateful for the wonderful doctors at Children's Hospital in Boston who cared for his daughter. When he left he said goodbye with a wave. He was looking forward to the evening because he and his son were playing their guitars and singing together at their church.

I realized after Louis left that he had been smiling the entire time he was working and telling me his story.

—My story

Each day you have the opportunity to explore ways of finding greater meaning or purpose in your work and life, just as things are at this moment in time. Your sense of purpose comes from doing what is part of your value system, not from what someone else wants you to do (we'll discuss this more in Chapter 8, "Create Goals and a Vision"). Someone in marketing can get a sense of meaning from developing consumer awareness of a useful product, as can a surgeon from performing complex procedures. In fact, it's how we look at what we do that makes all the difference.

TAKE A MINUTE

`00:01:00` What do you do now, or what have you done in the past, that is meaningful to you? It doesn't have to be work-related—just something that fully absorbed your concentration and that gave you a sense of purpose.

Following are ways to create greater meaning in your job now:

- Look for projects or assignments that will give you a sense of adding value. You may have to propose something to your boss. For example, if you think your company would benefit from a project that uses your skills, you might make a proposal that shows the time, resources, and benefits of doing so.

- Choose to mentor someone. It's a great way to pass on your knowledge and help someone succeed.

- Seek to partner with others who complement your skills so that you can focus on doing what you are best at. This will allow you to spend more time in what is called flow by positive psychologists—where you are fully engaged and time goes by without your noticing it.

When you search for meaning, keep the following in mind:

- The journey is as important as the destination. You make decisions based on the best information you have at the time. You can choose to look for the meaning in what you are doing at the present moment and find the lessons in it.

- We can find meaning in other areas of our lives besides work. For example, volunteering at a charity where you help others can be an extremely rewarding and meaningful experience. Or perhaps coaching soccer is meaningful to you because it is teaching young kids how to work together as a team, and you know that these are lessons that will help them throughout their lives.

WHAT WE APPRECIATE APPRECIATES

"If the only prayer you said in your whole life was,
'thank you', that would suffice."

—Meister Eckhart

Focusing on what you are grateful for is a powerful way to create a more optimistic perspective, which results in fewer health-related complaints and encourages more time spent exercising (a happiness booster in itself).

When you become aware of the good around you and learn to appreciate it deeply, you will have greater energy and focus and significantly increase your chances of success. You are also much more likely to behave in a collaborative way with others and reap the benefits of their goodwill.

How do you feel when someone says, "Hey, nice job"? I imagine you feel pretty good. So why not tell others when you think they've done a good job? The goodwill you receive will far exceed the amount of effort it takes to let someone know you appreciate his or her work.

I regularly send notes to people letting them know that they've done a great job, or that I am grateful for their efforts. I use a combination of e-mail and hand-written notes (the holy grail of notes). Frequently I send a note to someone's boss and copy the person. Both people appreciate the effort. I recently took a cardio clinic at my gym to learn how to use a cardio monitor during workouts. The young woman, Amy, who gave the clinic did a great job. At the end of the four-week program, I sent her boss an e-mail saying how much I appreciated the class. Both sent me back an e-mail of appreciation for taking the time to let them know what I thought of the class and of Amy's work. Now every time I walk into the club and see them, I am greeted with a warm smile. Nice.

STORY

SHOWING GRATITUDE BY SHARING

Over the years I have created a large database through networking activities and I've decided to use it. Whenever I'm going to a meeting, I think, *What introductions can I make?* At first it was awkward, but now it just flows. It's just so joyful. It comes easily. I consider it a win-win-win; a win for the people being introduced, a win for my company, and a win for my clients.

— CEO of a financial consulting company

TAKE A MINUTE

00:01:00 How could you help someone else? Can you make an introduction or give a referral? By helping others we are helping ourselves. We are showing our appreciation for their help and our willingness to, in turn, help them achieve their goals and dreams.

THE GRATITUDE JOURNAL

People who practice gratitude can increase their happiness level significantly. This is because by writing down three to five things that we are grateful for each day (before sleep or first thing in the morning), we start to focus on the positive things in our lives. And the more things we are grateful for, the more positive things we are bringing into our mental view (our consciousness).

I started practicing this during a particularly trying time. At first it was hard to think of anything that I was grateful for—all I could see were the things that were going wrong. But then I decided to just write down a few things that were working well. My husband and I were both healthy, our dogs (we have five) were also healthy, we have lovely neighbors— and suddenly things felt a bit lighter. I did this each night before I went to sleep for a week, and then something started happening. I realized that during the day I was noticing things like how beautiful the trees were in full bloom, how nice it felt when I walked to the mailbox and the sun hit my back. Small things, perhaps, but things I hadn't even been aware of before. They were right there, but I was so focused on the challenges I was facing that I didn't see them. And somehow by seeing them, I felt my burden lighten a bit. I was becoming more resilient.

What are you grateful for? It could be a bike ride with a friend, an hour by yourself to read a good book, or that the grocery store carries your favorite brand of ice cream. Nothing is too small or insignificant to warrant our gratitude.

TAKE A MINUTE

00:01:00 Each night before you fall asleep, make a list of what you appreciate in your job and in your life.

STRATEGIES TO INCREASE HAPPINESS

"If you don't like something, change it; if you can't
change it, change the way you think about it."

—Mary Engelbreit

SELF-INQUIRY

As we discussed earlier in this chapter, self-inquiry is a powerful tool. Through this simple process you can learn a lot about yourself and change what isn't working for you.

By becoming aware of what you are thinking and choosing to think something that is equally true but that makes you feel better, you can immediately alter what you are feeling. This technique takes a bit of practice, but it's a foundation for becoming happier.

When you are feeling something negative, ask yourself the following:

- What thought or thoughts were you having that caused the negative feeling?

- What is an equally true but different thought that makes you feel better?

DAILY WRITING

Write in a journal daily. Notice the negative stuff that pours out. Ask yourself if there is another way to view the same situation that would lead you to a better feeling. If so, what is it?

BUILD RELATIONSHIPS

Reconnect with old friends and family and build new relationships. People who are strongly connected to family, friends, and community enjoy greater happiness and health.

DO SOMETHING NICE EACH DAY

All you have to do to make yourself feel better is to say something genuinely nice to someone else. It doesn't have to be a big thing. For example, when you are checking out at the grocery store and happen to notice that the clerk has a new haircut that looks great, you might just mention it. I've done this and have been rewarded with a huge smile (and snappy service). People like to be noticed.

At work can you think of a way to tell someone that he or she has done a good job, without wanting something in return?

THE THREE-GOOD-THINGS EXERCISE

Martin Seligman from the University of Pennsylvania conducted a study of severely depressed people in which they were asked to write down three good things that happened to them each day. Things as simple as receiving a phone call or seeing the sunshine were recorded by the participants, who were so depressed that, in some cases, they could barely get out of bed.

The results were remarkable. Ninety-four percent of these "severely depressed" to "mildly to moderately depressed" people reported that they experienced relief within fifteen days.

THE POWER OF HABIT

A bit of effort is required when it comes to being happier. Repetition is required in order to make lasting change. When you learned to ride a bike, you had to practice. The first time you were on the bike, it felt awkward and scary (I am recalling, when I was a little girl, my father running behind me, trying to keep the thing upright). But after a while it became second nature, and you jumped on and rode without giving it a second thought.

The same happens when learning new skills in the area of personal growth. You need to practice—to create a habit—of using these skills. And once you do, they become a part of who you are and what you do.

Don't try to make too many changes at once. Select one or two things that you want to incorporate into your life, do each for between twenty-one and thirty days (the time it takes to make something a habit, depending on whom you talk to), and master them before you move on to the next.

GET MOVING

We all are aware of the value of exercise to our physical well-being. Now research is proving that it has a direct impact on our mental health as well. It improves cognitive functioning, it reduces anxiety and stress, and thirty minutes of aerobic exercise three times a week has been shown in some studies to be as effective as medication in reducing depression. WARNING: If you are on medications, DO NOT go off of them without speaking with your doctor.

KEEP A POSITIVE FEEDBACK FILE

This is a simple thing, but many of us forget to do it. Whenever you receive an e-mail or other written communication from someone saying that you did a great job or thanking you for your efforts, put a copy of it into your Positive Feedback file. You will feel great every time you look at the messages, and they will remind you of your achievements and recognized strengths. This file is also invaluable if you are someone who forgets how much good you've done because you are constantly focused on improving yourself or because you have an extremely high standard of excellence. This file will help you see that others appreciate your efforts and that you are doing great stuff just as you are now.

Keep your file in mind when you need references. These people have taken the time to show their appreciation for your work and would very likely be glad to give you a reference when the time comes.

We'll look at more strategies to increase your personal happiness and professional success in the following chapters.

TAKE A MINUTE

[00:01:00 What are some easy things you can do, or simple changes you could make, that would bring more satisfaction into your life?]

Happiness is something that can be increased by using specific strategies on a regular basis.

Career success is enhanced when you use these strategies because people like to work with people they like—and it's easier to like a genuinely happy person.

Happiness is not a panacea. Everyone experiences ups and downs. Resilience is the quality of being able to bounce back from life's difficulties and not get stuck in an emotional rut.

Select the strategies you want to incorporate into your life, and do one at a time for between twenty-one and thirty days until it becomes a habit.

3

Free-Range Emotions Tank Careers

"When dealing with people, remember
you are not dealing with creatures
of logic, but creatures of emotion."
—Dale Carnegie

WHAT WAS I THINKING?

Free-range emotions are like free-range chickens—
only dangerous. Unlike the lucky chicken who lives
her life roaming around the barnyard free to explore
at will and selecting food from various areas while
fraternizing only with the other chickens she likes
best, when our emotions roam freely, they can take

us into murky and potentially harmful territory. It's important to master your emotions so that you are in charge of what you say and do and how you behave at work. I'm not talking about becoming robotic—just capable of enough self-awareness so that you can choose to speak and act in a way that puts your best self forward at all times.

As we saw in Chapter 1, the strategy to do this is disarmingly simple. First, you must notice what you are feeling and then ask yourself what thought or thoughts preceded the emotion (and is therefore causing the emotion). That's the first part—getting in touch with what you are saying to yourself that is making you feel what you are feeling. Finally, think of an equally true but different thought that creates a better emotion.

This next story is a tale of a just such a scenario. A very successful person ran into a difficult situation resulting in an extremely painful experience—until she changed how she was thinking.

STORY

IT'S NOT WHAT YOU THINK IT IS

"I've finally had it," said my client, a senior vice president of a large international company. "I've decided to quit. Maybe it's just time to move on."

She had been in the position for about a year. It was a high-stress job because she was responsible for making extensive changes in, and to, the organization. In spite of that, she'd built an effective and loyal team in a relatively short period of time.

The hard work was not the problem. It was an unforeseen nemesis: a bully. A person of equal rank with a well-deserved reputation for going after and damaging other people. My client was just one on a long list of targets.

"He is spreading lies about me," she said. "He's ruining the reputation I've worked so hard to build—and no one can stop it. I'm not going to stick around and have everything I've done be ripped apart."

We had been talking about this escalating situation for several months, but it had obviously hit a peak. "What happened recently that was so bad you felt you had to resign?" I asked.

She paused. "It's one thing when he says something to me directly, either in a meeting or one on one. But last week he sent an e-mail with the most ludicrous lies about the program. Someone forwarded it to me. I felt like a hot knife was going through me when I read it. It was awful."

"So you think that people believe the stuff he wrote in the e-mail?"

"Yes. Well, I don't know. Maybe."

"So now you are a mind reader?"

"What do you mean?" she said tentatively.

"Would you believe something like that if you received such an e-mail about someone else, especially knowing that she is a solid performer and that he's a bully?"

"Well, no, I wouldn't."

"You've told me that everyone cuts him a wide swath because they don't want to become one of his targets."

"That's right. He's gone after so many people, but he's consistently made his numbers, so he's protected."

"Then why do you think that anyone believes him when he writes this stuff about you? Your peers can't defend you or he'll just come after them."

"You're right. Maybe they don't believe it, but it just makes me so mad that he can get away with this and no one can stop him. I've been working nonstop since I took this position and we've accomplished every goal that we set before the executive committee. This is just not right."

"I agree that it's not right. But the bigger issue now is that you are willing to resign to prove a point, or to make yourself feel better by stopping the pain. But I don't see that either of those things will happen. I do see that you'll be hurting yourself and the people in your organization who have worked hard right alongside of you to achieve so much in a relatively short period of time."

"What do you mean?"

"It might feel good at first to stop the pain, but after a while it's likely that you will wish you'd stayed and finished the battle. It's just human nature. If we run from a challenge, then we are doomed to continually play it out in our heads. So the real question is how to proceed. Shall we focus on that?"

This was an extremely painful situation for my client. My heart went out to her because these kinds of challenges have ruined many careers.

"Okay, but if I knew of a solution, we wouldn't be having this conversation," she said.

"I know this is very difficult for you, but you are making it much harder on yourself than it needs to be."

"How's that?"

"Because of the way you are thinking about the situation. Here's the thing: How we feel is a direct result of our thoughts. So, in your case, you are thinking that people believe the stuff this guy is saying, right?"

"Well, you've made me question that."

"Okay, but before our conversation you believed it."

"Yes, I did."

"And what was going through your mind when you thought about the situation?"

"Well, I thought that people didn't care enough about me to defend my reputation and accomplishments."

"And how did that make you feel?"

"I guess it made me feel hurt, sad, and a bit angry."

"Right. Now we can see that the thought—people don't care enough about me to defend my reputation—makes you feel hurt, sad, and even angry."

"Yes, it does."

"So what is another equally true thought that would make you feel better?"

She was quiet for a moment and then said, "Well, I can see that my peers just can't do anything about it without putting their own careers in jeopardy, but they have been warning me about what he's saying behind my back, and that shows they care."

"Good!" I said. "So how do you feel when you let yourself think in that way?"

"It doesn't make all the pain disappear, but

it does remove the hopelessness I was feeling. I see what you mean."

"This is what we humans do," I said. "Our thoughts are mostly unconscious. They run endlessly through our minds, and as a result, we often have feelings and emotions that are detrimental to our happiness and productivity. So, when we can grab the thought, question its validity, and consciously choose to think something that is equally true but positive, we feel better. And when we feel better, we are more optimistic, and we can put our energy into solving problems rather than just staying stuck in them."

"I get it. I really get it."

—Conversation with a vice president of an international computer company

Over the next several days she questioned her thoughts, evaluated their impact on her emotions, and came up with equally true yet positive thoughts to replace them. She repeated the positive thoughts whenever the negative thoughts arose. When she returned to work she knew that the battle was still in front of her, but she didn't feel that the outcome was predetermined. She felt stronger and better able to face the situation. She could see that the bully was just one person, someone who had lost his credibility, and as painful as his behavior was, she was determined to keep focused on building a strong and successful organization that would speak for itself through results.

This story has a happy ending. She stayed focused on replacing negative thoughts with positive ones— and the guy was fired.

It turns out that she was indeed a terrible mind reader. All along not only were her peers warning her in order to show their solidarity and desire to help her, but her boss and his peers were working behind the scenes to fix the problem altogether.

TAKE A MINUTE

`00:01:00` Think of a situation in which you felt helpless, angry, or frustrated. Now try to recall what you were thinking at that time. How did your thoughts lead to the emotions you were experiencing?

Most of us don't have such dramatic and challenging situations. Even so, work has inherent stressors, and it's how you choose to think about them that can greatly improve or derail your ability to handle them. Yet handle them you must or run the risk of spending enormous amounts of energy and time worrying about things that you've done or said. Of course, we all (or most of us anyway) can look back at a time when something came out of our mouths that we wish hadn't. That's life. We aren't perfect. But if you lack the ability to manage your emotions, then you are likely to run into trouble more often than you would otherwise.

For example, you might think, "No one sees how much I do around here," and that makes you feel sad, angry, frustrated, fearful, jealous, insecure—you pick the emotion. Now you are in an emotional hold and you are likely to respond from that emotion. If you are angry, you might speak in an angry, or at least unpleasant, tone to those you come in contact with, possibly damaging a relationship with someone that you will have to work with for a long time to come.

For anyone with emotions (and, hey, if you are alive, you have them), all your hard work can fly out the window with a single inappropriate outburst. Developing an awareness of your negative thoughts and actively changing them to equally positive thoughts will put you in your emotional driver's seat.

In the story about my client, we can see that through questioning her automatic thoughts and deciding that they just weren't in her best interest and then by replacing them, she was able to better handle a very difficult situation. That is key to our being successful at work, because most jobs are filled with challenges—and it's how we respond to them that makes all the difference, both in our careers and in our personal lives.

HOW ATTITUDE SHAPES OUTCOME

"Misery is a communicable disease."

—Martha Graham

Attitude is the outward reflection of what's going on internally (in our heads). A negative attitude is caused by negative thoughts, and we now know that negative thoughts lead to negative emotions, which usually lead to negative outcomes.

Your attitude is one of the most obvious and telling characteristics you possess. People may not be able to read your mind, but they certainly can read your attitude.

Having a negative attitude at work is like wearing a sign on your back that says "Don't Listen to Anything I Say," because that is ultimately what happens. Negative people get tuned out (unless two negative types get together, and then it's a negativity lovefest).

I interviewed executives and managers for this book and they had a consistent response to this question: What are the strongest attributes of new hires straight out of college? The answer was enthusiasm, energy, and positive attitudes.

TAKE A MINUTE

`00:01:00` Could you benefit by improving your attitude at work? If so, how would you change it, and how would it benefit you to do so?

Let's take a look at another story that plays out in organizations every day.

STORY

THE STONEWALLER

"What's up?" said Tyler, not taking his eyes away from his computer screen.

"Well, uh, Dwayne needs an inventory report of all the departments right away," said Curtis, standing outside Tyler's cube with a stack of folders under his arm.

"He gets a quarterly report. Why can't he use that?" *More to the point, why can't people leave me alone so I can get my work done?*

Curtis shifted his legs and moved the folders to his left arm. "Because he needs to get a supply chain analysis to Toni by Friday and it has to be based on the most current numbers."

"These guys just make work for themselves, and us. I haven't got time for this," Tyler said, finally looking up at Curtis. "I can't get you the latest numbers until next week," he said, turning back to his screen and thereby signaling that the conversation was over. He knew he was being a pain to Curtis, who wasn't a bad guy, but he didn't want people thinking that they could just dump work on him whenever they felt like it.

What do people think I am—a machine? If I don't push back, they'll keep demanding more and more from me, thought Tyler.

"Listen, Tyler, I know you're busy. We all are. But this isn't optional. There's a meeting with the steering committee, and Toni needs the most current view of the business and Dwayne has to get it to her."

"This is endless. No one has any idea how much work goes into getting these numbers,"

Tyler said, making a sigh that sounded more like a grunt. "I'll have to run this by Beth. If she takes something else off my plate, I can get you your numbers."

"Okay. When do you think you'll talk to her?"

"She's tied up in meetings all day, so maybe sometime tomorrow."

"Right. So the earliest you could have the numbers, if she approves you doing it, would be by when?"

"I don't know. I'll need to get current inventories from all the department managers and review them with Beth before I give it to you. Friday at the earliest."

"But the entire report is due to Dwayne by Friday."

"Listen, Curtis, this is the best I can do," said Tyler, shuffling through a stack of papers on his desk, his back to Curtis.

"Okay, but all the other departments will have their reports in by end of day tomorrow. I'll go with what I've got and let Dwayne know that you need to talk with Beth before you can do anything."

"Yeah. Let the two of them work it. I'm not jumping through hoops just to get numbers to people that they already have."

—Curtis and Tyler, two people in every company

Have you ever been in Curtis's shoes, trying to do something and having a difficult time getting someone to respond to your request? Are you inclined to voluntarily work with that person again?

Tyler doesn't want to do what Curtis is asking. On one level he is right to run the new request by his boss, Beth, before he takes on something that could derail his current assignments. But from his first sentence it's clear that he has no intention of trying to get his department's current inventory numbers to Curtis without creating a delay. He is annoyed by the request. His tone is negative: "These guys just make work for themselves, and us. I haven't got time for this." He doesn't try to figure out a way to help Curtis.

Tyler is stonewalling. He knows that he will have to get Dwayne the numbers. But he's annoyed at being asked and wants to make it as difficult as he can for Curtis.

Why is Tyler behaving this way? Maybe he thinks it gives him control over his work and an opportunity to show his boss how overworked and valuable he is. Or maybe he's arrogant and thinks that he's smarter than everyone else. Whatever the reason, the outcome is the same: His colleagues avoid him if they possibly can and the managers in the department have pegged him as a whiner.

Now let's take a look at how this could have played out differently.

STORY

THE STONEWALLER—REVISED

"Hey, Tyler. Got a minute?" said Curtis, standing outside Tyler's cube with a stack of folders under his right arm.

"Hey, Curtis. What's up?" Tyler said, turning away from his computer screen to look at Tyler.

"Uh, well, Dwayne needs an inventory report of all the departments right away."

"What about the last quarterly report?"

"It's not current enough," said Curtis, shifting the folders from one arm to the other. "There's an executive meeting and Toni needs to present the latest numbers. Dwayne has to get them for her."

"Okay. When do you need our inventory numbers?"

"End of day or early tomorrow would be great. I have to pull all the departments' numbers together, and then Dwayne needs to do a supply chain analysis and give the whole package to Toni by 5 p.m."

"Wow, that's tight. I'm working on something that I need to get out today, but let me give Beth a call and see if she can wait a day so that I can work on this for you and Dwayne. She's in a meeting, but I'll e-mail her—she checks regularly and usually gets back quickly."

"Great, Tyler. I really appreciate this. I owe you one."

"No problem. I'm sure I'll need the same from you soon enough."

In this scenario Tyler didn't roll over because of Curtis's request. He showed appropriate interest and gave a realistic and helpful response. He let Curtis know that he understood the urgency of his request and that he'd have to get it approved by his boss. And he gave a timeline for getting her input. Curtis was left with the sense that Tyler would do his best to meet the request, and he also left with a positive feeling about working with Tyler again in the future.

TAKE A MINUTE

00:01:00 Write about a time when you encountered someone with a negative attitude. What happened? How did the person's attitude affect the outcome of your interaction? What do you think would have occurred if he or she had had a positive attitude?

A CHANGE IN ATTITUDE

"It is our attitude at the beginning of a difficult undertaking, which, more than anything else, will determine its successful outcome."

—William James

Changing your attitude takes desire. You have to want to do it. Many people have a weak attitude toward work. They simply show up. They aren't fully engaged. The reasons (excuses) are many, but the end result is the same: a lukewarm attitude and a lukewarm career. If you are just going through the motions because you think that the work, the company, your boss, and your peers aren't worth your full engagement and attention, well, you've just written the script for how things will play out. You are in control of your attitude and the results it brings you.

This next little story illustrates how you might help yourself develop awareness about your attitude by enlisting someone you trust.

STORY

ATTITUDE-FREE ZONES

One summer my niece was visiting for a week. She was ten at the time, and she could be moody. I thought a lot about how to deal with her emotional roller-coaster rides in a way that would be positive and productive. Finally, I came up with the idea of an attitude-free zone.

After she arrived and got settled, I said, "Hey, guess what?"

She looked at me with a bit of suspicion and said, "I dunno, what?"

"This is an attitude-free zone," I said cheerfully.

Her face scrunched up a bit as she tried to figure out what on earth I was talking about. "What do you mean?" she asked.

"Just what I said. No attitude allowed this week. If something is bothering you, you can tell me and we'll deal with it," I said, smiling. It took her a few seconds, but she got what I was saying. She jumped up and ran into the living room to find her father. "Daddy, guess what? This is an attitude-free zone," she said as though she'd become the keeper of an important new concept.

—My (and my niece's) story

Only once in the entire week did I have to remind her gently that we were in an attitude-free zone. When I did, she took a few minutes to collect herself and then rejoined the group as if nothing had happened. She was her happy little self again.

Try implementing an attitude-free zone for a weekend at home, with your friends, or at work for a week with sympathetic colleagues. Gently let each other know when their "attitude" is showing.

The point here is that we can change the way we think and, therefore, how we behave. The more in touch we are with our thoughts, the more we can analyze them and choose to think something that is more productive and healthier.

FIND THE GOOD IN OTHERS

"I don't like that man. I must get to know him better."

—Abraham Lincoln

Looking for the good in others makes developing a solidly positive attitude a lot easier. If you think that most people are bad, then it is almost impossible to develop a strong social network, which is a key component of increased happiness and career success.

If you think that others are dumb, lazy, untrustworthy, or worse, you need to take a good look at what that kind of attitude is doing for you. For example, how does feeling that way help you? Does it keep you feeling superior? If so, why do you need that? Does it act as a buffer between you and others so that you don't have to get close to them?

Career success requires the ability to get along with others, so if you believe that people are intrinsically difficult to get along with, it's going to be tough to build the contacts, relationships, and reputation that will support your goals. This is an attitude worth trying to adjust. And the benefit is that once you start seeing the good in people (at least more often than you see the bad), it makes you happier.

A great way to develop a regular habit of looking for the good in others is to simply hang out with other people who do just that. I am married to some-one who sees the good in everyone. He's not blind to people's faults, but he doesn't go looking for them either. It's rare for him to be critical of someone else. He sees people as interesting, and he delights in get-ting to know them. What an attitude to be around day in and day out!

TAKE A MINUTE

00:01:00 Is there someone you could look at in a new and more open way? If you did, what would happen? How would your relationship change? How might you feel?

THE BRING-VALUE MENTALITY

This is a story about four people named Everybody, Somebody, Anybody, and Nobody. There was an important job to be done and Everybody was sure that Somebody would do it. Anybody could have done it, but Nobody did it. Somebody got angry about that, because it was Everybody's job. Everybody thought Anybody could do it, but Nobody realized that Everybody wouldn't do it. It ended up that Everybody blamed Somebody when Nobody did what Anybody could have.

—Author Unknown

A bring-value mentality is about being of service. We ask ourselves questions such as, *What is needed here? How can I be most useful? What skills do I have that I can put to use?*

With a bring-value mentality you are thinking about what you can do that would be valuable to your company, to your boss, to your peers, and to yourself.

People who are genuinely interested in others, are willing to be helpful even without getting directly or immediately rewarded, look for solutions to challenges, and focus on getting things done in a win-win manner are of great value to their employers.

This is a foundational characteristic of naturally happy people. They pay it forward by helping others to do well, and they know that they will receive the rewards when it's their turn.

TAKE A MINUTE

00:01:00 When does your attitude slide into negative territory at work? What are the triggers? What can you do when one occurs to keep yourself in a positive-attitude state?

CHAPTER HIGHLIGHTS · CHAPTER HIGHLIGHTS ·

When you are veering off course emotionally, ask yourself: (1) What am I feeling? (2) What thought(s) preceded the emotion? and (3) What would be an equally true but different thought (that my brain would believe) that would make me feel better?

Your attitude speaks volumes. In fact, it starts sending messages the moment someone meets you or you walk into a room. If the signal you send is negative, then over time people around you may simply tune you out.

Cultivate a bring-value mentality by looking at what you have to offer that someone else could benefit from.

PART TWO: SUCCESS TRAITS

"I have become my own version of
an optimist. If I can't make it through
one door, I'll go through another
door—or I'll make a door. Something
terrific will come no matter how dark
the present."

—Joan Rivers

4

Pragmatic Optimism

"I am an optimist. It does not seem
too much use being anything else."

—Winston Churchill

A FUNDAMENTAL TRAIT

A fundamental trait of happy people is that they are
optimistic. They see the possibility of success, where
the pessimist sees only opportunity for failure. But
what is optimism, and why it such a desirable trait
in a professional? Is it because no matter what happens you can always look on the bright side? Is it that
optimists never give in and keep on going no matter

what happens? And if so, why are those desirable traits? Wouldn't a good dose of reality about how many problems there are and how hard they are to solve be a better approach?

We've all heard the old sayings about looking on the bright side and seeing the glass as half full. But until late in the last century, we had little scientific proof that people who were optimistic fared any better than the rest.

Imagine that you could change your level of optimism and that by doing so you would be able to bounce back more quickly from life's setbacks. Further imagine that with this confidence and resilience you could take on greater challenges in your career and grow professionally because you're willing to stretch yourself. Finally, imagine that because of all of this you find yourself becoming a happier person.

The need for this information has never been greater. Rates of depression are increasing worldwide. We are in a time of great change, with new demands, multitasking requirements, and more decisions regarding purchases than ever before. We are in need of tools to help us cope, and thrive, in a world that is very different from just a few decades ago.

Cultivating optimism helps you deal with the many forces poised to derail your happiness and success both at home and at work.

Here's a story of someone who made a conscious decision to become an optimist.

BECOMING AN OPTIMIST

I wasn't always optimistic. I had to learn how to be so. My family was of humble means, and my mother did not even have the right to vote when I was growing up in Switzerland. I loved books, but at that time there were not libraries like the ones we have here in the United States, and my parents did not have enough money to buy them for me, so I would read the same book over and over again. Also, being a girl, my parents thought that my education was not as important as that of my two brothers.

As a young adult, I moved here, to the U.S., learned English, married, and had three children. Many years later, after finding the strength to get a divorce, and I was on my own with my kids, I got my undergraduate degree followed by an MBA. It wasn't easy, but I loved learning and was thrilled with my education.

Over the years I rebuilt myself—my self-esteem and self-worth. I now know that I have both the smarts and the resilience to change course if necessary. I surround myself with people who believe in me. When I decided to start my business, I just began asking people to be on my advisory board, or to be an ambassador for my company. I'm a risk taker. Almost everyone said yes.

The company launch was great. People were giving me input and saying, "I wish I had the guts you have."

I've met three times with the board. They aren't paid. They say, "We believe in you. We want you to succeed", and that they get a lot out of being part of this team.

My upbringing did not prepare me for this kind of success. Life did. I wanted more and I worked on becoming an optimist, and from that place, I've been able to succeed in ways I couldn't have imagined in the past.

—CEO of a financial consulting company

This terrific story illustrates how, over time, someone became optimistic through focus, dedication, and work. She says that she had to learn to be an optimist, since, due to the circumstances of her birth, it did not come naturally to her. But she did it, and with such wonderful rewards.

TAKE A MINUTE

00:01:00 When have you overcome an obstacle in your life? How did you do it? How did you feel afterward? Did it make you feel more optimistic that the next time you encountered a challenging situation you could handle it?

WHAT OPTIMISM IS AND WHY IT WORKS

"The young do not know enough to be prudent, and therefore they attempt the impossible—and achieve it, generation after generation."

—Pearl S. Buck

I used to think that you had to be born an optimist— that some people just were and others weren't. In fact, it is true that some people are more naturally optimistic than others, and some more pessimistic. But if you weren't born a natural optimist, take heart. You can become more optimistic. Here are the benefits you will receive:

- Optimists see bad situations as being temporary and isolated, as opposed to the pessimist, who views the same situation as being long lasting. People who are optimistic see life's difficulties as temporary setbacks, that each situation is unique, and that difficult situations are challenges to be overcome.

- Optimists are more likely to take the most hopeful view of a situation. This keeps their minds open to possibilities for solutions—a critical career skill. I was once in a meeting where a group of senior executives were bemoaning all the challenges they faced in a particular division. They went on, each weighing in on the direness of situation. Finally, the leader piped up and said, "Well, in good planning session style, we know what the problems are. Now, does anyone have a solution?"

We are faced with challenges every day. Those with the presence of mind to think of solutions are of great value. Optimists are resilient. They take hits just like everyone else, but they bounce back more quickly than those who are less optimistic or downright pessimistic.

Pragmatic optimism is not about putting your head in the sand and thinking everything is rosy when it's not. It's about believing that you will find a solution or you will finish the project or you will get

whatever you need to get done when you need to—
because you've done it before and you'll do it again.

Given the number of challenges we face at work—
sales targets, strong competition in the marketplace,
an increasingly difficult to influence customer, office
politics, and an endless array of other forces—we
would render ourselves inert if we were pessimistic
about the majority of these challenges.

TAKE A MINUTE

```
00:01:00
```
Think of a time in your life when you were optimistic and how it affected the outcome of a situation.

ADDING PRAGMATISM TO OPTIMISM

Pragmatic optimism is what we have when we com-
bine a can-do attitude with realistic perspective. It's
the kind of optimism that comes from knowing that
all we'll get from being pessimistic is a loss of appe-
tite for doing the work that needs to get done.

Before I go any further here, let me say that there
can also be valid arguments for taking a pessimistic approach. Martin Seligman explains in *Learned
Optimism* that there is a place for both optimism
and pessimism in business. If you're a CEO, you want
your marketing and salespeople to be optimists and
your finance people to be pessimists. This is because

in terms of finances you don't want to risk failure (I'll avoid the obvious cryptic comment about how a few financial services leaders would have benefitted from this idea before the recent economic crash).

So, yes, if you are lining up a crane and a wrecking ball, you don't want to be overly optimistic that it will hit the intended target. A bit of healthy pessimism will ensure the alignment is checked and rechecked before pulling the lever that sends the ball crashing into the structure. But if you are not in the businesses of finance or taking down buildings, then pragmatic optimism is a valuable skill to have.

In *Good to Great,* author Jim Collins relates a story about Admiral James Stockdale, who was a POW in Vietnam from 1965 to 1975. When the author asked Admiral Stockdale who did not make it out, the admiral said that it was the optimist.

Stop. What? How could that be? And why would I include this story in a chapter about pragmatic optimism?

The answer lies in what Admiral Stockdale told Jim Collins.

He said that the optimists didn't survive because they had unrealistic expectations. They kept giving dates, by next Christmas or by Thanksgiving, for when they would be released. Eventually, since they were interred for many years, they eventually "died of a broken heart." On the other hand, those who had faith that they would eventually be released— and did everything they could to stay alive in the meantime—survived.

Pragmatic optimists see the difficulties in front of them and are realistic about how hard something might be, but they look for solutions and they do what it takes to get to a positive outcome.

TAKE A MINUTE

`00:01:00` In what area of your career could you take a more optimistic view of things?

CHAPTER HIGHLIGHTS · CHAPTER HIGHLIGHTS ·

Pragmatic optimists are not blind to the difficulties and challenges they face. However, they see them as temporary, whereas the pessimist sees them as lasting.

Optimism that is grounded in reality is a core trait of naturally happy people. They are optimistic in the face of challenging situations, they see the obstacles, and they do what it takes to surmount them.

Cultivating pragmatic optimism will enable you to have greater resilience in your career and life, and therefore spend more time being happy than you would otherwise.

5

Take Responsibility

"We are made wise not by the recollection of our
past, but by the responsibility for our future."

—George Bernard Shaw

IT'S ALL OR NOTHING

Over the years I've worked with a lot of people.
Many of them were extremely smart and talented
and in most ways a real pleasure to work with. However, there is one distinguishing factor that would
always emerge—usually sooner than later—and
that is a willingness to take full responsibility for
whatever happens in his or her career. Those people

who possessed that trait set themselves apart very quickly.

Here's what happens when you take full responsibility for yourself:

- You recover quickly from difficulties (we'll see this in an upcoming story).

- People learn that they cannot push your buttons because you simply own up to something and propose a workable solution.

- You can take on other kinds of responsibilities more easily, such as managing other people.

- You are more likely to get what you want.

- People like working with you (and for you).

- You become much happier.

In the late 1990s I was working at a start-up consulting company. It was the height of the Internet bubble, and we were enjoying the ride. I headed several practices, and my staff and I were responsible for managing large client engagements, up to $100 million in revenue.

My clients were executives of some of the largest companies in the world. Imagine their surprise when they met me for the first time. In my suit and heels I stand 5'2", and I was responsible for the outcome of some of their most important initiatives, the ones that they had already announced to Wall Street, the ones that could impact their stock value.

In order to do this work, I had to take complete responsibility for everything that happened on a job. If someone on my team made a mistake, I owned it, and I owned fixing it. No excuses. My clients didn't hire us to hear why we couldn't get something done or why we had screwed something up. They hired us to do what they could not do on their own and they wanted it done right. Here's a story about just that situation.

THE BUCK STOPS HERE

Once, during a very large engagement, one of my staff members made a significant error. My mistake was that I did not catch it immediately. The result was that I quickly found myself in a conference room with a group of unhappy clients. The conversation rapidly digressed to an exploration of all the horrible things that could happen because of the error.

After several minutes I interrupted and said, "I understand that we have a problem—and I understand that I own it. I have a plan that I'd like to propose in order to get us back on track." They were quiet, so I continued, "If you accept this plan, we will start to execute immediately. After we are stable, if you are not satisfied in any way, my company will make you whole on whatever you've paid us for which you think you did not get value." I held my breath and waited, watching for a response.

Fortunately, everyone agreed to hear the plan. At the end of my proposal, they all agreed with the approach, and we got the process in place that same day. The team did an outstanding job of correcting the problem, with the damage under control quickly and completely resolved within far less time than we had estimated.

Our client received daily updates on the situation, and never once did I have to field an angry call or e-mail.

Finally, in order to make good on my promise to reimburse payments if they were not happy with the outcome, I went to see the CFO. I reminded him of my promise and asked if he wanted to discuss financial adjustments.

He looked at me and with a wry smile said,

"That won't be necessary."

—My story

Why is taking responsibility for what happens at work so important, especially since so many people clearly don't? And why should we take responsibility when we can't control much of what goes on anyway? Isn't it just plain dumb to blame ourselves for things that happen beyond our control?

Well, the answer to the last question is, yes, it would be destructive to blame ourselves for things that we had absolutely nothing to do with. However, many times we simply choose to ignore our own behavior and, therefore, how it gets in the way of our success.

TAKE A MINUTE

`00:01:00` When have you taken full responsibility for yourself at work? What happened? How did it affect the outcome and how did you feel?

Here's another story:

WHAT'S IN A NUMBER?

> My client and I were walking to get lunch. It was midyear review time, and the managers were trying to finish up meetings with their staff and submit the written reviews.
>
> As we rode the escalator to the cafeteria, she told me about one particularly perplexing situation. An employee had been rated a 4 (1 being the highest and 5 being the lowest performance rating). That meant he'd met some, but not all, of the requirements for his position. His manager was counseling him on ways he could improve his performance for his next review. After some discussion he finally said, "Well, if you want me to be a 1, you have to pay me like a 1."
>
> Things went downhill from there for him.
>
> —My story

Talk about not taking responsibly. This guy was writing his own ticket to a frustrated and unhappy career. This is a bit of an extreme example perhaps, but it's not uncommon for people to blame others for their lack of career success. But blaming someone else for what happens in your career is like giving someone else the keys to your car and telling them to drive it for you. If you do that, wherever you wind up is up to them—not up to you.

In your career you have faced many challenges. Maybe you aren't being recognized in the way you think you should be, or you don't have a great relationship with a key person in the office, or the work has just become stale and you're bored. It's up to you what you choose to do with each of these challenges. You can give up, complain, or be generally unhappy— or you can devise a strategy that will make you think and feel differently about the situation.

Tal Ben-Shahar, professor of the Fundamentals of Positive Psychology course at the University of Pennsylvania, speaks eloquently about the concept of practical optimism. He describes the concept by saying that happy people use techniques to make themselves feel that way and that they understand that what they create in life is up to them—no one is coming. No one is going to swoop in and save him or her, like in the movies. The beauty of this is that by taking this approach—by being completely responsible for their lives and careers—they take seriously the job of steering the ship to where they want it to go.

When you take responsibility, you can grow professionally and personally. When something doesn't go the way you want it to, it's an opportunity to learn, make adjustments, and do it differently the next time because you will ask yourself this question: *What did I do to contribute to this situation or event?* Maybe you didn't complete an assignment on time or you weren't as helpful as you could have been when someone asked you for something, or maybe you were just thinking that the person asking you was not worthy of your best effort.

When you explore how you contributed to an outcome that you didn't like, you can then determine how you will do it differently next time. You can envision the outcome you want in the future and then work to create it with your new insight.

In this next story we see how someone took responsibility for an outcome that might happen.

STORY

WHAT'S THE WORST THAT CAN HAPPEN?

When I started the company twenty-five years ago we were doing graphics. I engaged printers to work for me. They would do the printing, and I would bill the client for the work, the client would pay me, and then I'd pay the printer.

At one point the amount owed to the printers was $60k. This was a huge sum in my mind at the time. I'd never seen an invoice for $60k, and I started to worry, *What if the client doesn't pay me. How can I pay the printer?* I was filled with fear.

Then the thought came to me that if I couldn't pay the $60k, I'd go to work for the printer and work off what I owed him. I'm great at sales and I could bring enough in to pay for whatever I owed him. Suddenly I wasn't afraid anymore. In fact, I thought to myself, *Bring it on—$100k, $200k. I can handle this.* And, of course, I never had to go to work for the printer and have been in business for twenty-four years since.

—President of a branding and design firm

TAKE A MINUTE

`00:01:00` Can you take more responsibility for your career? If so, how would you do it? What do you think would be the outcome?

CHAPTER HIGHLIGHTS · CHAPTER HIGHLIGHTS · CHAPTER HIGHLIGHTS

By taking responsibility for your career, you can steer it rather than be steered by it.

Naturally resilient people take responsibility for themselves. Their perspective is that no one is coming to save them, so they better do it themselves.

When you take responsibility for your failures, you can grow from them. If you don't take responsibility for them, you just get to keep repeating them.

6

Focus on Your Strengths

"Some of the best business and nonprofit CEOs
I've worked with over a sixty-five-year consulting
career were not stereotypical leaders. They were
all over the map in terms of their personalities,
attitudes, values, strengths, and weaknesses."

—Peter Drucker

PLAY TO YOUR STRENGTHS

There are two views on strengths: one focuses on
what you do well (or test well on), and the other is
centered on what you naturally enjoy doing. I believe
it's necessary to think about both because sometimes

we are good at something, but it's not what we would enjoy doing all the time. I'm a pretty good cook, but it's not something I want to do all the time. I'm also very good at managing complex programs, but I find that I most enjoy the early stages when there are a thousand things that need my attention and I can create order out of chaos. But once the structure is in place, I get bored.

In Chapter 1, "What Happiness Is and Isn't," we saw that the second level of happiness is engagement. When we are fully engaged in an activity, hours can go by but it seems like minutes. We've become lost in the experience. As mentioned in an earlier chapter, this is what psychologists call flow.

A characteristic of naturally happy people is that they focus on their strengths. It makes sense if you think about it. Rather than beat themselves up all day for what they aren't naturally good at doing, they focus on positioning themselves to do more of what they are good at. By doing this, they experience more positive thoughts, leading to more positive emotions and, hence, greater happiness.

If you are not clear on what your strengths are, simply pay attention to what you enjoy doing and what others tell you that you do well. If you are in sales, you may get energized when you are talking to a prospect. If you are in marketing, working on a new campaign may be where you lose yourself for hours in the work. Just notice what you like doing during the day.

I have a friend who loves prospecting. She gets excited when she's about to meet someone for the first time and discuss his or her needs and how her company might help him or her. So she tries to spend as much time as possible in this role and have her talented employees do the development and delivery of the contracted work.

Most educational systems focus on improving the student's area(s) of perceived weakness. If she is good in math but only moderately capable in English, an emphasis will be placed on bringing her test scores up in English. The objective is to get good grades in all subjects. On the surface this makes sense, but there is an unintended consequence, which is that it can create adults who focus more on improving their perceived areas of weakness than on finding ways to spend more time in their areas of strength. This can lead to a never-ending stream of negative thinking, which leads to painful emotions and lack of energy. From this depleted state, many people simply don't have the desire to try something new that they might enjoy doing.

As we just discussed, you can do something about it if this has been your experience. Many hard-working and successful people are dissatisfied, but they are not sure why. It may be that they are doing only what they are good at and not enough of what they enjoy doing.

This next story illustrates how one bright woman changed the pattern.

CHANGING THE GAME

I used to obsess about improving my areas of weakness, but all it did was make me feel inadequate. In graduate school I was introduced to the concept of focusing on strengths, and it inspired me. I realized that all I was doing was depleting my energy.

My strengths are in seeing the big picture, so when I had to do highly detailed work, I was miserable. It wasn't that I couldn't do it, but I would obsess about getting it done and waste time. So when I started a new job, it was great to find someone who was outstanding at details. We worked together for several years, and we made a great team because we were both able to work in areas of strength, so we were happier and highly productive.

I use this approach all the time now. I always look to find someone with skills that complement mine.

—Manager of an international consulting company

Perfect! She figured out that although she was capable of doing the detail work, she didn't enjoy it. But because of her drive to do things well, she would drive herself crazy getting everything done but be miserable while doing it. So she looked to partner with someone who loved doing what she did not.

When I first worked for IBM, I had a partner. It was common for people to work in teams, and I lucked out. What was so great about our situation was that he was very technical and loved getting into the weeds, and I was more interested in the business application of the technology. We worked together for several years, naturally divvying up customers and projects. It was a win-win-win: he won, I won, and our customers won.

FINDING YOUR STRENGTHS

A few years ago I was at a crossroads. It wasn't the first time, but this particular experience led me to seek a new approach to my work.

I took the tests offered by two very helpful Web sites: Clifton StrengthsFinder 2.0 and the University of Pennsylvania's Authentic Happiness, which together revealed a picture that made sense and shaped my thinking for how I wanted to direct my work in the future. (See Resources at the end of this book for URL links.)

The UPenn VIA Survey of Character Strengths is made up of twenty-four traits. After taking the free online test (you must register), you will receive an instant electronic report that shows you which of the twenty-four are your top five strengths, and then lists the remaining in rank order. In his book *Authentic Happiness,* Martin Seligman provides further information on each of the twenty-four characteristics.

Here's how this test helped me. Of the top five characteristics in my results, the first one was Appreciation of Beauty and Excellence. Now take a look at how Dr. Seligman describes this characteristic in *Authentic Happiness:*

> You stop and smell the roses. You appreciate beauty, excellence, and skill in all domains: in nature and art, mathematics and science, and everyday things. When intense, it is accompanied by awe and wonder. Witnessing virtuosity in sports or acts of human moral beauty or virtue provokes the kindred emotion of elevation.

What an eye-opener this was for me. I suddenly realized that if I wanted to become happier, I needed to spend more time smelling the roses—and at the time I wouldn't give myself five minutes to leave my office and go for a short walk.

Notice that this particular character strength crosses nature and art, mathematics and science. This put my career and my life in better perspective: in my professional life I started as a systems engineer and then moved into management of large IT organizations and programs, and in my personal life I love being outdoors.

Armed with this information, I realized that not only had I been dipping into each of these areas, but more importantly, I didn't have to give up one to focus solely on the other.

In his book *StrengthsFinder 2.0*, Tom Rath includes thirty-four strength themes. When you take the online test (you'll need a key that is in the back of his book to do so), you will get an instant report with your top five themes and ten things you can do to maximize them.

The top theme in my results was Strategic. Here's an excerpt from the book that describes what that means:

> The Strategic theme enables you to sort through the clutter and find the best route. It is not a skill that can be taught. It is a distinct way of thinking, a special perspective on the world at large. This perspective allows you to see patterns where others simply see complexity.

This was another piece of the puzzle to what my strengths were and what I simply did naturally. No wonder I was able to turn around multimillion dollar technical and business programs that had gone badly off track. Within a very short period of time,

I could see what was wrong and what we needed to right the ship. It was just obvious to me.

Through these tests I realized that if I were to reach my goal of becoming happier, I had to filter everything I did through a new lens that included what I did naturally well, what I enjoyed doing, and what I got paid to do.

GO EASY ON YOURSELF

When it comes to finding your strengths and then finding a job or career that allows you to spend time doing those things—well, it can take some time. Please don't beat yourself up if you aren't doing something you love by some arbitrarily set date. The important thing is to point yourself in the direction of figuring out what (a) you are good at and (b) you really like doing. Then look for situations where you can spend more time doing those things rather than those you don't do as well or don't enjoy doing. Also, look to collaborate with those who complement your skills because they like doing what you don't.

TAKE A MINUTE

[00:01:00   Describe a day
                 (real or imagined)
in which you did mostly what you both
enjoy and are good at doing.   ]

CHAPTER HIGHLIGHTS · CHAPTER HIGHLIGHTS · CHAPTER HIGHLIGHTS ·

Focusing on your strengths means looking both at what you do well and what you like doing.

To increase your happiness, seek out opportunities to spend more time doing things you enjoy doing and that provide a sense of accomplishment when you do them.

Also, seek out others who complement your skills. Together you can each spend more time doing what you individually enjoy and, as a team, have the complete set of skills to do a great job.

7

Build Your Team

"And time for reflection with colleagues
is for me a lifesaver; it is not just a
nice thing to do if you have the time.
It is the only way you can survive."
—Margaret Wheatley

BEYOND SOCIAL NETWORKING

Studies show that people with lots of social connections are happier than those with only a few intimate relationships. This is because they have a large group from which to draw for support when they need it. In essence, they create a large social "net" work—like the net below a trapeze artist.

In our careers we have many opportunities to create relationships that will sustain us for years to come. But too often we find ourselves sitting behind a desk, sending e-mails or leaving voice mails, rather than getting out and meeting our coworkers.

STORY

IN THE FOXHOLE

I am fortunate to work in an organization with extremely talented people. But given the fact that most come from engineering backgrounds and we are in a highly technical business, it's easy for people to fall into the trap of working for years with others but never getting to really know them personally. Instant Messenger, e-mail, and conference calls are business accelerators. But you do not build trusted personal relationships among people using these electronic methods. You need to build these relationships in good times so that when a challenge arises, you can immediately focus on solving the problem and not on having to establish trust. So I now tell everyone who works for me to leave their desk and go meet the people they are working with. Make the extra phone call. Go have a beer after work. Get to know the person. Because when the battle comes—and it will—you want to know that the person in the foxhole has your back and understands who you are and what commitments you mutually share.

—Senior director of an international technology corporation

If you are shy, it can be uncomfortable at first to step out of your personal space. But this is important if you want build the kinds of relationships that can make your career more productive and successful. When you do, it can result in lasting benefits to you and to those in your network.

YOUR TEAM MEMBERS

"It is amazing what you can accomplish if you do not care who gets the credit."

—Harry S. Truman

Today you need to be more fluid than ever when it comes to shaping your career, given how quickly things change. In this section we look at the kinds of people you would do well to look for as part of your team. You'll notice that I've included social networking sites, but it's at the bottom of the list. That's because although I believe that these services are extremely valuable, first and foremost we need to get out of our cubes or offices and create in-person relationships.

THE MASTER MIND GROUP

This is a simple but powerful concept that has been practiced by business leaders for a long time and that you can benefit from no matter where you are on the ladder. It's made up of two or more (usually not more than five or six) people who come together on an agreed-upon schedule. Each person, in turn, shares wins for the period and then a summary of what he or she is focusing on or what he or she needs input from others on. It's important that each person have an equal amount of time to speak. Of course, occasionally someone may need a bit more time because of a particularly challenging situation, but as a rule, the group will work best if each person feels he or she has gotten time to be heard.

The beauty of this kind of group is in its simplicity and effectiveness. It provides support by the fact that each person has a place to air his or her experiences, but it is highly focused on one thing—achieving one's goals. It's not a place to vent, although some of that may occur. It is really a venue to help get done what would be hard to do on one's own.

PARTNERS AND BUDDIES

Either formal or informal, having a partner or buddy can be a huge boon for your career. He or she can provide input in a safe and direct manner, and over time, the more you trust one another, the deeper the learning can go for each of you.

The words (partner/buddy) are less important than the objective and results. What you are looking for is someone you trust with a similar perspective to yours. The point of the relationship is to work on whatever you both think is important at the time.

When you are looking for a buddy, here are the things to keep in mind:

- Select someone of similar temperament and goals.
- Have specific things that you want to work on.
- Agree on how you will work together.
- Agree on how you will handle sensitive subjects should they arise.

These relationships can be priceless, so make sure that you both are clear on what you want to accomplish and how you will communicate. The more open and relaxed you can be, the better.

MENTORS

These advisors have walked the path before you and willingly share what they've learned. They give advice and counsel to the mentee, who benefits from their experience. In return, the mentor receives the satisfaction of passing on hard-won experience and helping a willing learner.

Is there something you would like to be mentored on? Can you think of several people you'd like to have as your mentor? If so, make a list of these people and contact them with your request. Let them know that you value their time, that you are asking for no more than fifteen minutes every four to six weeks, and that you will come prepared with specific questions that you'd like their input on. If someone says no, don't be discouraged, just move on to the next person on the list. Be persistent and you will have a relationship that can benefit both of you for many years to come.

TAKE A MINUTE

`00:01:00` Who would you like to be your mentors? List their names. Call and ask if they would be willing to mentor you for fifteen minutes a month.

COACHES

Unlike mentors, unless asked, coaches do not dispense advice. Coaching is forward-moving and future-focused. The work is on achieving professional and personal life goals, and the emphasis is on action, accountability, and follow-through.

When you work with a coach, you are the driver, and the coach, in essence, sheds a light on the path in front of you. You will set the agenda for what you want to accomplish in each session, and you will sign up for action steps after each meeting that will help you achieve your goals.

Being coached can be a life-changing experience because it is a time for intense (or not so intense) self-discovery in a safe and comfortable situation. Many coaching sessions are held on the phone, so the time can easily be fit into a busy schedule.

PROFESSIONAL CLUBS

There are thousands (probably hundreds of thousands) of professional clubs. Depending upon their purpose, they offer opportunities to meet people, hear speakers talk about a variety of topics, or attend workshops to build your skills.

Choose a club that provides activities for professional development based on your objectives, and plan to be an active participant in order to get the greatest value. Call people in the club and invite them for coffee or lunch. Ask them how they use the club and what advice they can give you for getting the most out of it. Always ask how you might provide value to the club, and to them.

SOCIAL NETWORKING SITES

I'm a great believer in social networking—used wisely, of course. I'm on LinkedIn, Twitter, and Face-book, and I have a Web site (www.gerath.com) and a blog (www.gerath.com/blog). These are all great and are useful for keeping in touch with the latest news and thinking on various topics.

The most important thing about using these sites is to know what you want to accomplish with them. Do you want, for example, to establish a professional presence, or are you using them for a combination of personal and professional purposes? If the latter, it's important to make sure you've secured the site so that nothing inappropriate appears when a career contact finds you.

Give yourself a great gift and choose even one of the above relationships that you want to cultivate now.

The next story highlights how social networking can help not only your career but also your personal life.

THE REVITALIZED NETWORK

For a long time I let my network languish. I focused on my job and on my relationship with my husband. It took a divorce to wake me up to how much I'd been missing.

Now I use Facebook for what I call the light-touch contacts—people I went to graduate school with, for example. I have reconnected with former colleagues and classmates, and it's great to keep up with what they are doing. I can let people know if I'm just returning from a trip, and that might spark a conversation.

At work I have an inner circle of people I need to stay in touch with regularly. For this I've learned to schedule half-hour meetings. Maybe we just get coffee, but since we've scheduled meeting time, we are sure to get together, and this keeps communication flowing and issues can be resolved quickly.

I heard once that you can't have more than ten people in your inner circle. I don't recall where I heard it, and I don't stick to it rigorously, but it does cause me to think seriously about who I need to give my time and energy to, because I only have so much of each.

Beyond that inner circle, I envision other outer layers of connections and how I will keep in touch with people, and how often. It sounds a bit calculated perhaps, and it is. But without doing things this way, I used to just let relationships fall, and I no longer do that. They are all too valuable to me.

—Manager of an international consulting company

NURTURE YOUR NETWORK

"Talk to a man about himself and he will listen for hours."

—Benjamin Disraeli

A client of mine says that she a rule of three: She does three things a week that advance her career but are not directly related to her job. These include contacting people or reading something related to her industry. She uses this rule to make sure that she reaches out to her network on a regular basis and is current on topics beyond her specific responsibilities so that she can keep up her end of a stimulating conversation.

Just the word networking sends shock waves of fear through some people. I used to be one of them. The idea of having to find interesting topics to speak with someone about made me a wreck. Then I learned this:

Don't talk about yourself; ask questions about the person you are speaking with.

The point is that people like to talk about themselves. When you are interested in someone else (rather than trying to be interesting to them), you've made a connection. The conversation will flow more naturally and you can relax, and enjoy, your new contact.

If you have business cards (and hopefully you do), don't be shy about using them. I give my card to every new business contact. If I'm in a meeting, I take the opportunity to introduce myself to people before the meeting starts, hand them my card, and ask if they have one. Easy. I do the same at a luncheon where I am meeting new people. All this information then goes into my contact management system.

Be sure to put your contact information in your e-mails. This way people can put it into their contact system. They may not take the time to look up your information if you don't provide it. Your objective is to know people and be known.

You will need to follow up when you meet someone. This is the key to good networking. If you meet someone in a meeting and want to reinforce the good experience, send a note saying that you enjoyed meeting him or her and look forward to seeing that person in the future. Get in the habit of following up within a day of meeting someone new and it will become habit. Networking specialists advise that you follow up within twenty-four hours, while things are fresh in both your mind and your new contact's.

Through networking I have had the pleasure of meeting talented, thoughtful, and successful people from all across the globe and in almost every industry. These people have made my professional life far richer than it would be if I just sat in my office and wrote, consulted, or coached.

You might think that because of the coaching and consulting I meet lots of people and therefore don't need to network. Well, I do meet lots of people, but one of the ways that I do is through networking.

And, if at all possible, get together with someone versus just talking on the phone. People are growing huge networks through tools like LinkedIn and Facebook, but nothing creates a more lasting or substantial connection than meeting someone in the flesh. And remember to always ask someone with whom you are networking what you can do for him or her.

The key to networking is to do it regularly and be clear on how to use your time, and your new contact's time, while making the connection. Think about what you want to accomplish during the meeting, how you would describe what you are doing now, and what you want to do in the future. Get comfortable speaking easily about your professional strengths (no need to be boastful—just making simple statements about your abilities helps others understand what your capabilities are). Always thank people for taking the time to meet with you. And finally, send a follow-up note within twenty-four hours stating your appreciation for the meeting—and add a line or two of the key things you got from speaking with them.

Do this regularly and you will be far ahead of the pack in terms of building a strong network foundation. You will be surprised how quickly this network will grow.

STORY

BUILDING A VIRTUAL TEAM

In 2004 I went into business for myself. Before that I'd been in companies where there were always lots of people, meetings, and conference calls. I traveled regularly to work with clients, so in addition to the people that I managed and my bosses, I was in regular contact with people from my varied clients.

After about four years, I realized that I missed having lots of people around to bounce ideas off of, brainstorm solutions, and pretend that we weren't gossiping. I was perfectly happy otherwise. So I decided that I needed to build a virtual team that would give me, and the team members, the kind of stimulation and support that we would have if we were in larger groups. The question was, how was I going to do it?

The first step was to make a list of people who might be interested in this idea and could benefit from being part of such a group. I wanted a few close trusted advisors.

Not too long after I made this decision, I was at a conference where I met two people who have since become part of my team. It was like magic—or maybe not, because it turned out that they were looking for exactly what I was. We agreed to talk once a week on the phone, focus on our wins (what had gone well that week), and then discuss anything that we were working on that we needed help with.

These relationships have led to several more, and I now have a growing team of people with whom I speak regularly. We get excited about each other's accomplishments, and we help each other clarify our goals, stay on course, and secure resources or solve challenges when necessary.

—My story

TAKE A MINUTE

00:01:00 What have been your most effective networking experiences? What happened and why did it work so well?

Build your network by meeting face-to-face as often as you can.

Create a team of people who can help you. Find mentors, buddies, coaches, and mastermind members, and nurture those relationships.

Make networking a top career priority.

Help others. They will willingly help you in return.

8

Create Goals and a Vision

"If you aim at nothing, you'll hit it every time."

—Author Unknown

WHERE DO YOU THINK YOU'RE GOING?

If you don't know where you are going, you are likely to wind up someplace that you'd rather not be. Setting goals makes you think through what you want and how you plan to get it.

How can goals make you more successful, and happier? What magic do they hold that can change the course of your life? Why bother writing down what you want anyway? Don't you just have to live with whatever comes your way?

The reason goals are so powerful is because of the concept of the self-fulfilling prophecy, which means that what we think about is what we create. This concept has been widely discussed and taught in the self-help industry for many years, and now positive psychology research has shown the value as well. In addition:

- Having a set of goals allows you to enjoy the good feeling of having direction. This creates a sense of freedom to enjoy the journey because you know where you are headed and how you intend to get there.

- Pursuing and achieving stretch goals is a great self-esteem builder.

- By pursuing your goals, you continually learn and grow. For example, you may need to find resources to help you achieve a goal. This is an opportunity to grow in your ability to research, request, negotiate, or navigate new territory— all of which becomes part of a broadening knowledge base that you take with you into the future.

TAKE A MINUTE

[00:01:00 When in your life have you had goals, and how did they help you achieve a desired outcome?]

THE POWER OF GOALS

Goals focus the mind and create direction. Think of someone you know who seems aimless, going from one thing to another with no sense of direction or purpose. Without goals you end up roaming without a destination, taking whatever life and work presents. With goals you can significantly increase the likelihood of achieving, or acquiring, what you want. When you do this, it increases your self-esteem and self-confidence.

ALIGN YOUR GOALS WITH YOUR VALUES

Your goals should be based on what you value and want, not what you think others want for you or what other people value. If you choose goals that are not true to who you are, two things are likely to happen: (1) you won't follow through or (2) you'll follow through but your sense of achievement will feel hollow.

Your goals should be based on your values and what is meaningful to you. If making money is meaningful to you because you want to move to a good town with a good school system for your kids, then that is what is important to you at a deep level and will keep you focused.

To get to your goals, you will need to do a bit of homework, because it's important to look at your life as a whole when you determine what it is you most want to do and where you will put your time and energy. The table that follows is a good place to start. It has eight areas in which to set goals on the left side. In the middle is the goal (or the goals—you can have multiples in each area), and on the right is a place to write the date by which you plan to achieve your goal.

Having a date for your goal is important. Without it, goals can become something amorphous, the thing you'll get to when you get a chance to work on it. And we all know what happens then—we never get around to it.

So take some time in a quiet place and think about these areas of your life. What is it that you most want for each of them at this time? Pay attention to what it is that you want, versus what you think others might want for you. Try to make sure that your goals are based on the former.

GOAL SETTING AND TRACKING TEMPLATE

AREA	GOAL	DATE
Career		
Finances		
Health		
Friends/Family		
Significant Other		
Personal/Spiritual		
Recreation		
Physical Environment		

As you can see, this covers a lot of territory. But it is not necessary to have an equal number of goals in each category. If you are highly focused on work right now, and that's okay with you, then the other areas of your life may be fairly light in terms of goals—for now. The value of this template is to jog your thinking a bit. When you create your goals, think about the following:

- Let yourself think about what it is that you really want to have and achieve.

- Have at least one or two stretch goals (one of mine was writing a book). It's through these that the greatest growth occurs.

- Think about what you have to do to achieve your goal (you can write out the steps separately), and then plan the date by which you will achieve it. Note: If you push everything out too far, you run the risk of not getting a sense of accomplishment.

- Make it fun. Get creative by typing up your goals using an interesting font and vibrant colors. You can print them out and frame them. Putting your framed goals on your desk or some other area where you will see them regularly is a great way to keep yourself focused on what it is you really want to accomplish.

A WORD ABOUT BALANCE

The concept of work-life balance is everywhere today. And it's a great idea. But I think that it is sometimes misunderstood. My view of work-life balance is that there is no perfect ratio. If you are a working parent, you might be stretched just to get the kids off to school, get to work on time, and then get home and put dinner on the table. So, in that situation, it's necessary to be realistic about how much time and energy you have each day. For the period of your life when you are raising kids, some, perhaps many, of your interests will get less of your time than they would if you didn't have children—and a job. So don't try to make each of the eight areas equal in terms of your goals. My own goals have evolved over the years, as has the amount of time that I spend in each area of my life. I am able to pursue goals in more areas than I was in the past, because my time is allocated differently now, based on choices that I've made.

BRINGING YOUR GOALS TO LIFE

If you just go through the exercise of listing your goals and then stick them in a drawer only to be looked at once a year, you are likely not to have the results that you want. In order to give your goals real power, you need to make a habit of looking at them every day. I keep mine by my computer. That way I am sure to look at them first thing in the morning and usually at the end of the day as well.

Beyond just looking at your goals, take a few minutes each day to visualize yourself achieving each goal. Imagine yourself—what you are doing and wearing, who you might be with, what the weather is like, where you are—when you achieve your goal. Research shows that this process affects the brain by creating neural pathways.

In addition, update your goals regularly. There is no point in keeping a goal that you no longer want or care about.

TAKE A MINUTE

[00:01:00 How could setting goals and visualizing myself achieving them help me?]

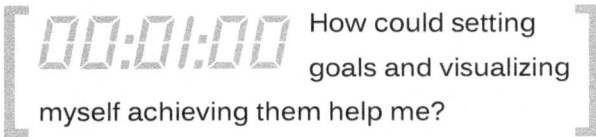

SEE YOUR SUCCESS

Sports coaches use the combination of visualization and practice to train athletes. First, this powerful duo creates a mental vision, complete with all the senses to make it as real as possible, and second, it brings the vision to life through movement. This is done not just for the real game but for all practices as well.

The same technique applies in your career. Before a presentation, for example, take a few minutes to visualize yourself giving your talk in a relaxed and lively manner. Do this several times, and by the time you present, it will be as if you've already given the presentation multiple times.

In the following chapters we'll look at additional time-tested professional skills for building a career—or redirecting one that has gotten off track.

Create your goals, put them in a visible place, and review them regularly.

Have at least one or two stretch goals. They are the source of growth.

Review your goals on a regular basis. Remove those that are no longer necessary or valid, and add new ones.

Visualize yourself moving through each and every step along the way to achieving your goals. Do this daily if at all possible.

PART THREE:
BIG-PICTURE SKILLS

"Two monologues do not make
a dialogue."

—Jeff Daly

"If it is not right, do not do it; if it is
not true, do not say it."

—Marcus Aurelius

9

Who's On First?

"A good listener is not only popular everywhere,
but after a while he knows something."

—Wilson Mizner

THE TROUBLE WITH TOO MUCH

Comedy duo Abbott and Costello's 1945 baseball sketch of Who's On First sums it up: not listening can lead to confusion—or worse. (If you haven't seen it, by the way, you can watch it on YouTube.)

In interviews I conducted for this book, lack of listening was a top concern for business leaders.

Here's the scene:

You've been invited to a meeting. It's one of way too many, but you accept it anyway and let it sit in your calendar. When the time comes, like a good soldier you show up, but you have no idea why you are there or what the objective is for the meeting. You don't know the host and haven't done any due diligence, and you decide to just zone out behind your laptop until it's over, figuring at least no one can bother you while you're there and you can catch up on e-mail. Then the host asks you a question and you've no idea what has been discussed because you haven't paid attention—and you don't know how to respond. You mumble something like "Could you please catch me up? I think I missed the last thing that was said." Ding!

Once you've learned to talk, walk, text, and do your job all at the same time, it becomes a hard habit to break. The problem with this is at least twofold: (1) it leads to inferior work because you cannot really understand what people mean if you don't listen to them, and (2) it sends a message to people that you aren't truly interested in what is being said.

How do you feel when someone puts down everything he or she is doing and sits quietly, focusing completely on you and what you are saying? For most people this kind of attention makes them feel like the other person is genuinely interested in who they are and what they have to say and they feel complimented.

When you give your full attention to someone, you are giving a great gift. You are saying to the person that he or she is important to you and you want to hear the person fully. Some people say that the gift of being present and fully listening to another person is the greatest gift we have to give. People like to be heard, and therefore, they usually like people who listen to them.

Here are a few tips on how to be a great listener:

- First, stop doing anything other than listening to the person who is speaking (whether in a meeting, on the other side of the desk from you, or at the dinner table).

- Focus on what that person is saying. If your attention wanders, try to bring it back to the other person.

- Keep mental tabs on the key points the person is making.

- In a one-on-one situation, state these key points as a way of (1) letting the person know you are listening and (2) confirming that you've heard correctly. Say something like, "What I heard you say is that we have to complete the project by Friday. Is that correct?" In response you might hear "Yes" or "What I said was that it would be best if we completed the project by Friday."

You need to be a very good listener if you want to build a strong career. By listening carefully, you will not only hear what is being said, you will also start to hear what is not being said. This is often where the real gold lies—and here's why: Very often people are not saying what they want to say, or think needs to be said, because they can't figure out how to do it without creating a problem. If you listen carefully, you can hear these non-statements, and then you can carefully probe to determine their validity. Once you know what the real issues are, you can craft an approach that can actually do some good.

GET TO THE POINT

"Nature gave us one tongue and two ears so we could hear twice as much as we speak."

—Epictetus

The ability to speak concisely is a gift that some people seem to have been born with. Everyone else has to practice. If you want to be heard, you need to be able to get to the point. With ever-shrinking attention spans, time, and patience, your words will have a much better chance of getting through the crowded space in the listener's head if you make them succinct.

TAKE A MINUTE

$00:01:00$ In what situations would you like to speak more concisely? How would it help you to do so?

Following are some ways to help you get to the point:

- Determine your general purpose (to inform, to influence, to inspire, to contribute, etc.).

- Determine the specific points you want to make.

- Decide what supporting material (information) is needed to make your point.

In other words, think about it and plan it out. Write down the key points and prepare in advance how you will present them.

At first this may be a bit cumbersome and you might worry that you'll forget what it is that you want to say. If that's the case, keep the points on an index card, in a notebook, or on your PDA or smartphone. However, once you've practiced this for a while, it becomes second nature and you will find yourself speaking concisely most, if not all, of the time.

Talk about a career enhancer. This skill and the ability to listen closely are two of the most powerful capabilities you can bring to work every day.

CHAPTER HIGHLIGHTS · CHAPTER HIGHLIGHTS ·

Listening is a lost art. Learn how to do it well and you will instantly set yourself apart and above most of the people you work with.

Being able to speak succinctly and get to the point quickly is the counterpart to (and enabled by) listening well.

10

Not Everyone Plays Nice

"You can't run away from trouble.

There ain't no place that far."

—Uncle Remus

STOPPING THE MADNESS

A number of years ago I had a client who had earned quite a reputation for being very hard to please. When I first met him he did nothing to convince me that he had been wrongly accused.

One day in the middle of a very large meeting, he started to rail about something that had been already been reviewed and resolved. I listened for a

few minutes and then said, "I hear what you are saying and yet we've been over this many times in the
past. Although I thought it was resolved, it appears
that I was wrong. Therefore, I suggest we end this
meeting right now and let everyone go. Then we will
get on the phone with the presidents of both companies so that we can resolve this for the final time.
Once we are in agreement with the go-forward plan,
we can reconvene this meeting."

You could have heard a pin drop. No one said a
word—including me. I just waited. Finally he said,
"No, that won't be necessary, let's continue," and the
meeting picked up as if nothing had ever happened.

What was the fallout for me? None. In fact, we've
worked together many times since, each time with
outstanding results.

Working with someone who challenges you (note
that I did not say working with a difficult person)
can be agony, or it can be a place of growth. Take a
look at this next story.

STORY

TURNING THINGS AROUND

> I was thinking about all the times in the work-
> place when we find ourselves working with
> people who, for whatever reason, we find dif-
> ficult. We don't like the interaction. They push

our buttons, we are depleted, angry, annoyed, power plays come in—anything like that. How many of us have just an arsenal of those situations to draw from?

The biggest shift I've made, and that I get faster and faster at as the years go by, is realizing that when I get hung up on changing the other person or really being in that judgment mode, thinking, *This is a nuisance. I can't believe I have to deal with this person,* I'm in a negative mode, and it impacts how I show up in the situation because it produces all this negative energy. So if I can remember to ask myself, *What do I get a chance to practice, learn, or experiment with as a result of this situation presenting itself to me?* instead of getting completely caught up in what I don't like about working with a person I think is difficult—if I can just remember to ask myself, *What do I get to practice here that will help me down the road*—then I shift into a more productive space. And usually with difficult people the answer is patience and tolerance. So it's like I get to expand my own skills and facility with those two qualities. If I can remember that, I start to value those interactions more and have a healthier outlook on the future interactions. *I'm going to practice tolerance in the next conversation. I'm going to practice being really curious about this other person who I clearly don't fully understand because I find them difficult.*

An example happened at my previous job where someone was micromanaging me. Micromanagement is a huge trigger for me. The issue was someone was micromanaging my approach over how I was going to do something to achieve a goal. When I was able to catch myself in the moment of feeling totally frustrated, and defiant and trapped— all of those things that are nothing but my resistance to doing it the way he was telling me to—when I caught myself feeling these things, I could stop and think *What is it that I don't understand here? What do I need to learn about why he wants this?* Then I could ask him, *What is it you get from this approach?* And then he was able to tell me enough about what he was looking for that I could go into alternative directions and get into a collaborative approach with him rather than having to just comply with a rigid approach that goes against all my values. I'm fluid and spontaneous and lean in the way I like to get my work done, which bumps me up against structured people all the time at work. It's a constant polarity that I have to manage everywhere I work and with everyone I work with because I'm so far on the flexibility spectrum (that continuum between structure and flexibility) that anyone's structure I encounter is an issue. I was dealing with someone who was highly structured and wanted to micromanage my own process. I didn't want to do it, and I was pissed. If I'd gone into compliance mode, the question was, *What was the quality they would get? What's going to happen to our relationship because I would be resentful?* Instead, I asked, *What is it you will get by using this approach?* Then I could ask myself what I can do to get that—without doing what he's asked me to do.

Especially when someone has positional power, that decision to stay in a creative tension is very challenging. Depending on who you are, how confident you are, how threatened you feel in your environment, you may find it challenging to take personal ownership and find a way to stay in the tension when it's really uncomfortable.

—Manager of an international consultancy company

A NEW APPROACH

"Eventually we will find (mostly in retrospect, of course) that we can be very grateful to those people who have made life most difficult for us."

—Ayya Khema

It's tempting to think that what when we find ourselves working with someone who challenges us, we need to figure out what is wrong with that person, or at least assess what type of person he or she is and adjust our behavior accordingly. But I've found that knowing myself is far more important than figuring out what will make someone else behave differently. After all, how well do you react to people trying to change you?

So what can you do when you're faced with having to work with someone you don't like or don't respect? To answer that, we will go back to the concept of self-inquiry, introduced earlier in this book. If you recall, by questioning what it is that we are feeling and then what thoughts we are thinking that cause the feeling, we can choose to think something equally true but different that makes us feel better. In the case of working with people we don't get along with easily, it is the first step to changing the way we engage with them.

> *Note:* If you are in a relationship where you are being physically or mentally abused, you should get out if it.

It's through this inquiry process that we can gain a clearer view of a situation, and construct and execute an approach that will be more productive than just going with our gut reactions (as we saw in Chapter 3, "Free-Range Emotions Tank Careers").

And it's through this process that we can start to put real teeth behind the often used statement "just don't take it so personally." How many times has this been said to someone who is in real emotional pain about a situation? In fact, it would be great to not take things personally. But how does one do that? How does one develop the ability to step back, assess, compose a reasoned approach, execute that approach, and deal with whatever comes next?

We need a process that allows us to accept our feelings and then move on to solutions. Too often people get stuck in their emotions, and that keeps them from moving past the pain and on to crafting a better outcome.

STEPS FOR DEALING WITH CHALLENGES

- Take a deep breath before you do or say anything. This simple step will allow you to be calmer and think more clearly.

- Remind yourself that the person is behaving in this manner because of who he or she is, not who you are. Each of us chooses at every moment (either consciously or unconsciously) to behave in a certain manner. If someone is behaving inappropriately, then that's his or her choice. You do not have to respond in a like manner.

- Ask yourself what you are feeling.

- Ask yourself what thoughts you were thinking that created the feeling.

- Now ask yourself what is another true thought that will allow you to feel better.

- If you are in a situation where you need some time, then excuse yourself by saying something like, "I hear what you are saying and I need a moment to think about it." A big part of dealing with challenging people is to not give up your power in the situation. Each of us has the right to be treated honestly and respectfully—and that includes you!

- Ask yourself what you need in this situation. The person in the previous story needed to feel she was participating in the approach, not being micromanaged. Because she was aware of this, she could ask her boss what it was that he wanted as an end result, and she could participate in crafting the approach. This gave her the sense of being part of the solution rather than just forced into compliance, which she finds extremely stressful.

- Develop a solution or alternative plan that you can present. Keep in mind that the best solutions are wins for as many people as possible.

- Take responsibility for any mistakes you may have made that are causing the person to challenge you.

- Do not be defensive.

- Know that you are doing your best in the situation, and give yourself credit for that.

TAKE A MINUTE

`00:01:00` Recall a situation that challenged you. Walk through the steps above. How might the outcome have been different by using this approach? How could you use it in the future?

Practice this approach, and over time, it will become a natural part of your approach to life. People who can step away from their emotional responses, evaluate situations, identify solutions, create consensus, and execute are extremely valuable in organizations.

GENERAL RULES
FOR BUILDING STRONG RELATIONSHIPS

- Respect others.
- Don't criticize others.
- Don't complain about people and don't gossip.
- See things from their perspective as much as you can.
- See the problem as separate from the person.
- Find out what is most important to the person in the situation.
- Never make someone lose face.
- Look for win-win solutions. (That means that you win too!)
- Develop a plan.
- Find a quiet location and lay out your plan to the person.
- Stick to the key points of your plan.
- Know in advance what you will concede to.
- Stay calm.
- Recognize the other person's efforts to find a solution, no matter how small.

CHAPTER HIGHLIGHTS · CHAPTER HIGHLIGHTS ·

Sticking your head in the sand is a poor strategy when it comes to dealing with people you find challenging because you will eventually stop respecting yourself for doing so.

Make every effort to understand where the other person is coming from, but not to the extent that you sabotage your own self-interest.

Speak clearly, without emotion, and do not place blame. Then stop talking and let the other person absorb what you've said.

Be willing to compromise—but not to be compromised.

11

Fun with Fraud
and Other Felonies

"I don't know nothin' from nothin' but

I do know right from wrong."

—From the movie *Erin Brockovich*

WHERE TO START?

This chapter is about having a strong moral compass to guide you through your career and your life. You might be wondering why such a topic is necessary in a book about career success and personal happiness. Good question. When I asked myself that question, the best answer I came up with was this: It's hard to be genuinely and lastingly happy and successful if you are behaving immorally or unethically, because it sets up a battle in your mind, a battle of competing thoughts, and that leads to stress and anxiety, or worse.

To start this chapter, we need some definitions. First, let's look at two words that we'll be using. These are from *Webster's New World Dictionary*:

Moral 1 dealing with, or capable of distinguishing between, right and wrong **2** of, teaching, or in accordance with the principles of right and wrong

Ethics 1 the study of standards of conduct and moral judgment **2** the system of morals of a particular person, religion, group, etc.

So, morality is having the capability to distinguish right from wrong, and ethics (in our case business ethics) is a system of morals. Don't you just love definitions? They make everything sound so simple, so understandable, and so clear. Unfortunately, when it comes to these two words, there is more than a small amount of room for interpretation—and that's where we start to get into trouble.

I believe that each day billions of people get up and go about their day with the intent to make an honest living, take care of their families, and be as happy as they can possibly be in their endeavors. But given that these kinds of stories get little air or print time, we are often confronted through news outlets with the worst of what we can be. And it's true that we are capable of some terrible behavior. But if we look more closely, we will find outlets that are reporting on the positive things that happen each day all around the world.

So where does this leave us? Are we good or are we bad? Do we even need a set of ethics, or should we just wing each decision?

I would argue that we are inherently good (although, in certain circumstances, capable of being bad) and that having a set of ethics helps us by providing guidelines for our behavior in challenging situations.

In business, in medicine, in politics, in education, in science, and in general, we are constantly faced with ethical decisions. How should we compete in the marketplace? Is it best to highlight the faults of our competitors or showcase our strengths? Is it better to rush a somewhat flawed product to market so as not to miss the seasonal buying window or to wait until all the bugs are fixed and potentially lose critical market share? Say, for example, you and a group of coworkers have worked on a project, but you believe that you've worked hardest. Do you deserve more credit than the rest and, if so, how do you go about getting it?

These are just a sampling of the kinds of situations that require a clear moral compass—an ethical code.

Let's break things down a bit further. Since this book is for you, the professional, we will discuss morals and business ethics from the individual's perspective rather than how a business should conduct itself (again, a subject for an entire book).

Having said that, I hope that after reading this section you feel inclined to start a conversation with others about how businesses can be both prosperous and have a strong moral compass. We are in a time of upheaval both socially and financially, which on the one hand can be viewed as a time of great upset and panic and on the other as a time of great opportunity for change. This change can come from the top, but it can also come from the center, and by that I mean all the people who make up companies. When there is a wave of social change, it can have a powerful impact.

PERSONAL AND PROFESSIONAL CODES

In your career you are dealing with both your personal code of ethics (based on your own moral code) and that of your employer. Most companies today have a code of ethics that has been developed to guide behavior and decisions across the organization. Again, this is not the place to question the implementation of those ethics by any individual organization (although suffice it to say that we've seen clear evidence that some do not practice what they preach). Many of the codes of ethics in business incorporate points such as the following:

- Impartiality and objectivity
- Full disclosure and openness

- Confidentiality
- Compliance with governmental rules and laws
- Avoidance of conflicts of interest (or the appearance thereof)

Of course, depending on the organization, there are variations on this theme.

It's important for you to know your organization's code of ethics. When a sticky ethical situation arises, the first place to go is this code. It is meant to provide a guideline on how to proceed. However, as we'll see next, there is also another code you will take into consideration.

YOUR OWN CODE OF ETHICS

Have you ever thought about writing your own personal code of ethics? If not, or if you've thought about it but haven't done it yet, I suggest you take some time and do so. Really. Here's a format that you can follow:

A PERSONAL CODE OF ETHICS—EXAMPLE

- I will tell the truth.
- I will take responsibility for my actions.
- I will treat others with honesty, respect, and dignity.
- I will be open to lifelong learning.
- I will be open to learning from others.

- I will share my knowledge for the good of others.

- I will give credit where credit is due.

- I will be true to who I am and not change myself just to fit in or to please someone else.

Your personal ethics are influenced by a variety of forces: family, community, and religious affiliation. By writing down your personal code of ethics, you are able to reflect on things that you might take for granted or that you want to highlight and focus on.

Following are some questions to ask yourself about your personal code of ethics:

- Are these mine or someone else's?

- Are they what I really believe?

- Are they in synch with my organization's code of ethics?

- If not, how do they differ?

- What will I do if I am faced with a situation where my personal ethics are in conflict with those of my employer?

TAKE A MINUTE

[00:01:00 Write down your personal code of ethics. Then write down your employer's code and compare the two.]

KEEP IT SIMPLE

Sometimes we make things more complicated than they need to be. Simplicity for some reason eludes us. For example, we have a nice little rule that sums up a whole lot of complicated issues. It is the basis of many religions around the world, and it's so easy to remember that it rolls off the tongue without so much as an extra neuron having to be fired in the brain. It's a marketing, public relations, and advertising dream, and it goes like this:

> "Treat others as you want to be treated."

Known as the Golden Rule, not only is this phrase easy to remember, it is also a simple concept to understand. It's like a filter through which to strain all our actions. Are we treating someone else the way we would want him or her to treat us? Is the action we are about to take something that we would benefit from if we were on the receiving end?

This little rule might be helpful to you when you think about writing your code of ethics.

STORY

A POSSIBLE SITUATION

You are in sales and your company has a policy against misrepresenting your competitor's products. This afternoon you have a meeting with a prospect who is in the process of deciding between your company's product and that of another company. You know the other company's product has a flaw because you've read about it in the newspaper and it's been on the television.

Since the information is publicly available through multiple sources, you might feel justified in pointing this out to your prospect. However, be warned that whenever you speak negatively about a competitor, it ultimately reflects on you. Although it may not be against your company's policy, your personal reputation is on the line. People remember such things, and when it comes to giving you slack when your product shows weakness, they may not be as willing to do so as they would have had you been more diplomatic toward your competitor. In other words, every time you sling mud at someone else, some of it gets on you.

—A common story

RECOVERING

People get tripped up about all kinds of things at work, often when they are just trying to do the right thing. Having a strategy for dealing with situations that have gone awry could save a whole lot of pain.

REALISTIC EXPECTATIONS

Years ago I heard an executive tell his employees to execute their jobs flawlessly. He wanted to inspire them to have high standards. The problem was that most of them already had high standards and telling them to execute flawlessly set a bar that was unrealistic. He did not tell them to stretch themselves to do better than they thought they could. He told them not to make any mistakes—ever.

Even the best and brightest people make mistakes. Even those with a strong moral compass and work ethic sometimes err. So the real point is this: Work to the very best of your ability, challenge yourself to do better than you think you can, and when you make a mistake, you will have the credibility you need to resolve the situation promptly and without damaging your career. Here's what I always told my staff: "Do your very best, but when you make a mistake, it's how you recover that counts."

THE ONLY WAY OUT IS THROUGH

When you make a mistake, here is how you recover:

- Own your mistake. Admit your error immediately.

- Apologize. Say you are sorry for what has happened.
- Ask what you can do to fix things. Executives need to do more than ask. They need to provide a solution.

We've seen example after example of CEOs who would have done well to take this advice. Without accepting responsibility for their mistakes, apologizing, and doing something to fix things, they have lost credibility. They have lost their moral compass. They blame others for mistakes that they have made, somehow thinking that their employees, shareholders, and the public will let them off the hook. But this is not what has happened. Don't follow their lead.

Most organizations have a code of ethics. Make sure you know what your employer's are.

Take the time to create your own code of ethics.

Evaluate your personal ethics against those of your employer's to see if there are any conflicts. Then evaluate what you would do if such a conflict arose.

Consider making ethics a topic of conversation with friends, family, and colleagues.

12

Change Happens

"Our only security is our ability to change."

—John Lilly

FEAR OF FLYING

It was a fine morning for flying. The sky was blue, the winds were calm, and the sun was streaming through the windows of the Seattle airport as my husband and I waited for the first flight out to Boston. It was the end of a wonderful and much-needed vacation.

We found a comfortable place to sit as we waited to board the plane, coffees and newspapers in hand. As I opened the business section of the *New York*

Times, one article jumped out at me: The organization I worked for at IBM had been sold to another company.

This is how I learned that the position I'd held for the past two years no longer existed.

Fortunately another position soon presented itself. I was relieved and threw myself into my work. Eventually, however, I left on my own terms. After twelve years of working for that great company, I gave in to my strong drive to pursue other opportunities, other experiences, other companies and clients.

Change can be devastating—and it can be enlivening. It all depends on how you choose to deal with it. I know that's a bold statement. This chapter is for those of you who don't like change and don't cope with it as well as you'd like.

WHEN THE WIND BLOWS

Change creates a state of transition, and transition causes imbalance until we're through it. Change and transition are also sources of tremendous personal growth both professionally and personally.

Right now we are in a state of great change because of the economy. Companies are consolidating, and layoffs are prevalent in a number of industries. And although there currently is inherent instability in many business sectors, even when this period is behind us, change will still be a force to be reckoned with. Technology, corporate "right-sizing," and outsourcing have altered the landscape forever. The old saying is that the only certainties are death and taxes. We need to add change to that list: The only certainties are death, taxes, and change.

I have been through many changes. At one point my husband and I both worked in the same department at IBM. In the 1990s the company was going through a huge downsizing. One day a large group of us were at a meeting at a local hotel. There we heard what a great asset each of us was and what a good job we had all been doing. Then we were told that our department was being disbanded. You could have heard a pin drop in the room.

After the meeting I called my husband, who was working with customers in Europe, and told him that he should think about spending a few more days there when he was done. He might as well get in some sightseeing because, as of that moment, neither of us had jobs.

We survived. In fact, we've both been through other significant changes in our professional situations since. Each time we've survived.

Whenever a change has rocked my world, I take a step back and look at what has been working for me in my current situation and what hasn't. What have I wanted that I was denying myself? How could I use this change, this transition, to get more of what I wanted? This is not always an easy process to do when I also needed to pay the bills.

DEALING WITH CHANGE

When change happens the first thing to do is let yourself experience whatever you are feeling. If you are afraid of it, so be it. Let yourself feel the fear—but not for so long that it paralyzes you. Give yourself a time limit on how long you are going to feel bad (say, one good night of being freaked out), and then in the morning, make a plan of what you are going to do. Start with what you liked about your current job and what you didn't like. Then make a list of what you want more of in your life and your work. Finally, write a detailed plan of what you have to do, and by when, to get yourself to where you want to be next.

You may not have a choice if your company decides to relocate and you don't want to go where it's headed, or your boss with whom you have a great relationship is being replaced by someone with the reputation of a tyrant. But you do have a choice as to how you handle the situation.

It's okay to feel unsettled when something is happening that will affect you in potentially unforeseen ways. It's not okay to let it take you to an unhealthy place mentally or to react defensively, complain, whine, badmouth others, and on and on.

You are going to choose your path, and since you will be choosing it, you might as well pick a good one.

To recap, the following are steps for dealing with change:

- Let yourself freak out if you must—but not for long. Give yourself a time limit and stick to it.

- Make a list of what was working for you in the current situation and what was not.

- Next, make a list of what you want more of in your life and in your work.

- Finally, write out as detailed a plan as possible of what steps you need to take, and by when, to get you to where you want to go.

A bit of a warning is warranted here because during this time it can be both helpful and harmful to enlist the aid of others. If you want company on this journey, be careful whom you choose. I've seen people who are still active in support groups years after a company layoff. The problem is that much of what occurs is commiseration. This can keep you stuck. Focus on finding people with a positive, get-it-done attitude.

Getting through a career transition is as much work as a full-time job. So if you give 100 percent to your job, then give that same amount of attention and energy to yourself while you are transitioning. Get up every morning and go to work. In this case you are your own client. Invest in yourself to whatever extent your situation allows. If money is tight, then libraries are a great source of free information about job hunting, career changes, and industry activities.

Recently I was working with a client, a very talented guy, who was in the midst of a difficult situation. He could stay in a job that he knew well, but that meant continuing to work for someone with extremely poor people skills (and I mean *extremely* poor). Or he could, in this difficult market, start to explore new job opportunities.

While on a walk with my dogs, I was mulling over his dilemma. As I walked, here's what popped into my head and what I told him:

- Look past the present (everything and everyone), and focus on what you want.

- Do what you need to do to get there.

- See yourself doing those things calmly and assertively.

- Speak clearly to everyone about what you want.

The point is that although from one very valid perspective we are much better off living in the present (a Zen philosophy to which I subscribe wholeheartedly), there are some times in our lives where the present is not worth dwelling on. Okay, that's a bit flippant so let me explain.

When we are facing a change, it is important to take stock of all the good in our lives (as mentioned, gratitude is one of the greatest ways to increase happiness). However, when things are really difficult, dwelling on the difficulties, how they've come to pass, why we can't fix them, and so on is simply a way of keeping ourselves in the quicksand.

Learning to let go of those thoughts takes some discipline, but it's important to do because you need all the energy you can muster, and if you are hitting yourself over the head with your emotional baseball bat, you're going to be too sore and tired to get up and do what must be done.

DON'T WAIT UNTIL YOU'RE IN IT

Here's the thing: You probably know deep down inside that change is inevitable and that at some point, no matter how comfortable (or anxious) you are, something's going to happen and you'll be experiencing an unsettled situation. The problem is that even though you know it, you might not be willing to think about it until it's fully on you. And when you are swept up in a life-altering change—say you lose your job—well, that's a tough time to start thinking about what you want to do and how you are going to do it.

When you're hit with a surprise change, it can be like being sucker punched. It takes the wind out of you. So my suggestion is that you start thinking about what you would do *if* . . . you finish the sentence. Don't wait until you are vulnerable. You've probably heard the old saying, "Expect the best but plan for the worst"—that's pragmatic optimism.

Following are some ideas on how to plan for change:

- Keep an inventory of your skills. Know what you are good at.

- Learn to speak about yourself as if you were a brand. Write down what makes you unique, and how an employer would benefit by having you on the team. Perhaps you are a go-to person who gets things done every time. Get comfortable saying that, or whatever it is that makes you a great asset to have around.

- Stay current with what's going on in your industry, not just in your company. Read articles in industry-specific magazines and e-zines. Frequent blogs that are well respected by your peers, and comment appropriately. Review industry white papers, and know who the key people are who are shaping your field.

- Help other people as much as you can. Provide them with references, give them information they can use when looking for a job, and make contacts that will enable them to achieve something that's important to them.

- Spend less than you make, if you can. We're a consumer society (although we can see how well that's served us lately). If you have some money in the bank, you will worry less when change happens.

If you keep these things in mind and practice them, you will be in much better shape to weather a storm than if you just allow yourself to coast until change comes knocking.

ANOTHER KIND OF CHANGE

"We spend our time searching for security and hate it when we get it."

—John Steinbeck, *America and Americans*

So far we've looked at change that occurs from the outside. Now let's take a look at what happens from within. It's the kind of change that happens when you no longer feel enthusiastic about what you are doing and you're bored. It might be that you are working too hard, or the things that you are doing have become routine and there is no challenge left. In any case, you are now in a state of discomfort and you need to take charge of getting yourself back on track.

BACK AGAIN

> I was sitting in the chair at my dentist's office reading a magazine and waiting for a cleaning and checkup. When the dentist arrived, he asked me what I was reading. "An article on burnout," I said. He looked at me and said, "Burnout. Yep. I've been there and back again."
>
> As he poked at my gums with his sharp, pointy tool, all I could think about was how glad I was that he was back again.
>
> —My story

TAKE A BREAK

Maintaining your enthusiasm takes a conscious effort. It requires breaking from work on a regular basis in order to give your brain a rest so that it can do its job better once you go back to work. Studies show that personal productivity increases when you take a short break every ninety minutes. I now do this and am amazed at how much more I can get done if I stick to this routine. It doesn't take much of a break either. All of us who spend lots of time sitting need to stand up and stretch regularly. We don't need sugary foods and caffeine to keep us going (although I love those things as much as anyone else). Try standing and doing a few simple stretches. Don't look at your computer screen while you're doing it either. Maybe read a few lines of a book that inspires you. Then get back to work.

Let me give you another example. I love doing crossword puzzles, although I'm not particularly good at them. Even so, I do one from the *Boston Globe* every day. When I first started doing puzzles I was easily frustrated if I didn't finish one—which was most days. Then I became obsessed with finishing the puzzle in one sitting, which became a time-sink. Finally I was able to get myself to just do as much as I could in twenty minutes and then leave it and get to work. At lunch I would pick it up again—and voilà—words that my brain would not produce in the morning were right there for the plucking at noon. Suddenly I could see that I was looking for a synonym to a word that had three meanings—but I was looking for a synonym to the wrong meaning. I had walked away from the puzzle, and when I returned, I had a fresh perspective.

INDULGE YOUR PASSION

Perhaps walking your dog or visiting with friends gives you a lift. You might find that time passes quickly when you are the movies, visiting art exhibits, watching sports, or reading. These things are often the ones that people let go of because of work demands. Slowly you stop doing the things that give you joy. Yet these are precisely the things that you need to continue doing or put back into your life if you've dropped them.

I'll say it again; I'm not talking about work-life balance. I'm talking about slipping a few things into your day or week that you really like doing. For me it's walking my dogs, both because they like it and I like it (and we all need the exercise). Sometimes it's a short walk, and I'll confess some days it's no walk. My goal is to walk five times a week with them, and we usually do.

I realized how important this is when I was speaking with a friend on the phone one night. My life at that time consisted of getting up at 3:30 a.m. on Mondays to catch a 6 a.m. flight to wherever my client was and coming home late Thursday or Friday night. I'd been doing it for a number of years. I didn't realize how much it had gotten to me until I heard my response when my friend asked me how I was doing. Suddenly I heard myself say, "I'm okay, but if I were dead it would be the same thing."

Can you imagine? Perhaps you can. I did not realize I'd given so much of myself to work that I had nothing left over. I didn't feel depressed. I simply didn't feel much of anything. That was a defining moment in my life. It was a wakeup call to me that I needed to find things that gave me joy and pleasure and meaning—and I'd better do it quickly.

Even if you are overscheduled, overcommitted, overworked, and overtired, I am still telling you to find one tiny little thing that gives you joy and do it regularly.

TAKE A MINUTE

00:01:00 Make a list of a few things that make you feel refreshed when you do them. How can you do one of these things on a regular basis?

Ultimately, as much as we seek stability and comfort, change is simply part of life. The more you can accept it, prepare for it, know yourself well, build a strong network, help others whenever you can, practice being grateful for the good things in your life, stay current in your field, and have goals that keep you focused, the better able you will be to both handle the change and potentially thrive when it occurs. I believe you can do all of these things—and more.

CHAPTER HIGHLIGHTS · CHAPTER HIGHLIGHTS ·

Change is the new norm (along with the old norms of death and taxes). You need to learn to embrace it.

Change can be a source of opportunity and growth.

When change occurs, make a list of what had been working for you in the previous situation and what had not. Then focus on moving toward a situation that has as many of the positive attributes as possible.

Keep yourself from becoming stale or burned out by doing one or two things that make you feel refreshed on a regular basis. These things can be as small as watering your plants, cleaning one drawer a week, or taking the dog for a walk on a regular basis (which is good for both of you).

A Parting Wish

My wish is that you become the best of who you are. Not the best that someone else wants you to be, nor the best that you think you should be, but the best from the bottom of your heart to the depth of your soul and to the tip of your brilliant head.

Happy travels,
Ruth

Acknowledgments

When I first drafted the outline for this book, I could not have imagined the experience that was about to unfold. By the time the first draft was done, it looked nothing like the original outline and most chapters had been moved so many times they could have been dizzy from the experience. I've been excited, humbled, exhausted, and exhilarated, sometimes all in the same day. What a ride.

This book would not exist without the many talented people I met along the way. Let me tell you about them.

Sherry Gordon, a mentor and friend who is also an author, gave me wonderful insights—and names. It was through Sherry that I met and began working with Joanne Slike, a gifted editor and one of the nicest people I have ever had the good fortune to work with. Thank you, Sherry, for your quiet guidance over strong French coffee at LaProvence. And thank you, Joanne, for your firm hand in shaping what I originally sent you into what *From Hired to Happy* ultimately became. I have looked forward to every conversation, and we've had many.

Paula Black showed up on the journey and immediately became the navigator and friend I needed. She nudged me to the east when I was moving too far to the west, steering me without my knowing it. Thank you, Paula, for sharing so openly what you've learned through publishing your own three books and working with clients over the years to develop their brands.

Stephanie Peacocke was generous with her time and feedback on the initial concepts. Thank you, Stephanie, for your insights and great judgment that helped me get this project off the ground.

To my sister, Deb Pike, who encouraged me to write the book from the very start; Linda Minkoff; Rudi Scheiber-Kurtz; Star Dargin; and to my cousin and dearest friend, Deb Gardiner; thank you all for your encouragement and support during our round-table meeting and many discussions afterward. I am grateful to all of you for your ideas and guidance.

Roni Boyles is a woman with huge talent and unstoppable energy. Thank you, Roni, for organizing a focus group and for mentoring me in the art of public relations. It's a pleasure to watch your career blossom.

A special thanks to Meghan Gardiner, who listened to my ideas early on and encouraged me to write; to my sister, Mary Ellen, who believed in me all along the way; and to Nancy Dickinson, who gave me gentle guidance during our many walks with our dogs.

Thank you to the following people who gave their time for interviews and input: Laura Alvardo, Dr. John Bowen, Richard Fleischer, Sheri Ispir, Todd Lamothe, Sara Larsen, Caroline Loughlin, Kelly Mann, Mary McHugh, Tamara Monroe, Vihn Nguyen, Marilyn O'Hearn, Beth Masterman, Rutu Patel, David Spinelli, Brendan Ward, and Sarah Wasdyke.

To my parents, thank you both for your consistent encouragement, for your dedication to learning, and for making me do my homework.

And that brings me to the one person I haven't mentioned yet—my husband, Chris. It's not that I couldn't have done this book without you; it's just that I'm not sure I would have. Thanks for telling me to do what I wanted to do, and then helping me make the space to do it. You are simply the most important person in my life.

About the Author

Ruth Gerath works with business leaders from Fortune 10s to emerging companies.

She started her career with IBM and later moved to a start-up consulting firm (that eventually went public) where she was the head of multiple practice areas.

In 2004 she started Gerath & Company to bring a highly collaborative and customized approach to working with clients.

Ruth lives with her husband, Chris, and their five dogs in their homes in Massachusetts and Maine.

Resources

BOOKS

Authentic Happiness: Using the New Positive Psychology to Realize Your Potential for Lasting Fulfillment, by Martin E. P. Seligman, Ph.D. (New York: Free Press, 2002).

Getting to Yes: Negotiating Agreement without Giving In, by Roger Fisher, William Ury, and Bruce Patton (Boston: Houghton Mifflin Company, 1991).

Good to Great: Why Some Companies Make the Leap . . . And Others Don't, by Jim Collins (New York: HarperBusiness, 2001).

Happiness: A Guide to Developing Life's Most Important Skill, by Matthieu Ricard (New York: Little, Brown and Company, 2006).

Happier: Learn the Secrets to Daily Joy and Lasting Fulfillment, by Tal Ben-Shahar, Ph.D. (New York: McGraw-Hill, 2007).

How to Raise Your Self-Esteem: The Proven, Action-Oriented Approach to Greater Self-Respect and Self-Confidence, by Nathaniel Branden (New York: Bantam Books, 1987).

How to Stop Worrying and Start Living, by Dale Carnegie (New York: Pocket Books, 1984).

How to Win Friends and Influence People, Reissued ed., by Dale Carnegie (New York: Simon and Shuster, 2004).

Learned Optimism: How to Change Your Mind and Your Life, by Martin E. P. Seligman, Ph.D. (New York: Vintage Books, 2006).

Outliers: The Story of Success, by Malcolm Gladwell (New York: Little, Brown, 2008).

Six Pillars of Self-Esteem: The Definitive Work on Self-Esteem by the Leading Pioneer in the Field, by Nathaniel Branden (New York: Bantam Books, 1994).

StrengthsFinder 2.0: Now Discover Your Strengths, by Tom Rath (Washington, D.C.: Gallup Press, 2007).

Thanks! How the New Science of Gratitude Can Make You Happier, by Robert E. Emmons, Ph.D. (Boston: Houghton Mifflin Company, 2007).

The How of Happiness: A New Approach to Getting What You Want in Life, by Sonja Lyubomirsky (New York: Penguin Books, 2007).

What You Can Change and What You Can't: The Complete Guide to Successful Self-Improvement, by Martin E. P. Seligman, Ph.D. (New York: Vintage Books, 2007).

Who Moved My Cheese: An Amazing Way to Deal with Change in Your Work and in Your Life, by Spencer Johnson, M.D. (New York: G.P. Putnam's Sons, 2000).

STRENGTH AND CHARACTERISTIC ASSESSMENT WEB SITES

In StrengthsFinder 2.0, Tom Rath provides an easy-to-use assessment program that allows you to find your unique strengths. With a key (found in the book), you can access the test at the Web site *www.strengthsfinder.com.*

At the University of Pennsylvania's Authentic Happiness site, you can take many tests that will give you insight into your strengths, interests, and characteristics: *http://www.authentichappiness.sas.upenn.edu/Default.aspx*

Index